D1600842

Don't Look Now, But Your Attitude Is Showing

Don't Look Now, But Your Attitude Is Showing

By
Dr. Raymond W. Barber

SWORD of the LORD PUBLISHERS

P. O. Box 1099, Murfreesboro, TN 37133

Printed and Bound in the United States of America

CONTENTS

1.
ATTITUDE OF SUPERIORITY

The foundational text for this series is:

"For as he thinketh in his heart, so is he."—Prov. 23:7.

My particular text for this message is:

"For I say, through the grace given unto me, to every man that is among you, not to think of himself more highly than he ought to think; but to think soberly, according as God hath dealt to every man the measure of faith.

"For as we have many members in one body, and all members have not the same office:

"So we, being many, are one body in Christ, and every one members one of another."—Rom. 12:3–5.

Don't look now, but your attitude is showing. The one thing that most influences a person's performance and function in word, in deed and in thought is his attitude. Webster defines *attitude* as "the disposition or feeling with respect to a person or a thing."

How is your attitude toward your husband? toward your wife? toward your neighbor? toward your parents? toward your children? toward your boss?

I read in an airport a little sign:

Go ahead—tell your boss man what you think of him and set yourself free.

Your attitude governs every phase and facet of your life. Your attitude will determine where you are in your spiritual life, in your business life, in your family life, in your social

1

life. It will determine how far you'll get in the business world or in the world of academics or in the world of spiritual things. The bottom line is this: your attitude will determine where you are in every area of your life.

When you look at a person, whether or not you realize it, you're looking at his attitude. Someone has said that what a person has been all the days of his life shows up in his face. So be careful lest you end up a dried-up, fossil-faced old grouch.

Mark your attitude. That's another way of saying you are not what you think you are, but what you

Mark your attitude.

think, you *are.* Your thoughts are translated into actions.

He was wise who said, "Sow a thought; reap an action. Sow an action; reap a deed. Sow a deed; reap a habit. Sow a habit; reap a lifetime." If you think positively, you will be positive. If you think negatively, you will be negative. If you think critically, you will be critical. If you think cowardly, you will be a coward. If you think bravely, you'll be brave. If you think weirdly, you will be a weirdo. If you think sarcastically, you'll be sarcastic. If you think truthfully, you'll be truthful. If you think honestly, you'll be honest.

The greatest verse in the Bible on mental therapy is Philippians 4:8 where the Apostle Paul says:

"Whatsoever things are true, whatsoever things are honest, whatsoever things are just, whatsoever things are pure, whatsoever things are lovely, whatsoever things are of good report; if there be any virtue…think on these things."

Attitude Makes the Difference

The reason people behave unsightly, unseemly and untowardly is that they think in those areas. Remember, your thoughts are translated into actions and deeds. When your attitude is right, your family relationships will be right, your homelife will be enhanced, your business will grow, your church life will flourish, your Sunday school class will increase. You will be thinking well about your friends, about your family, even about your enemies. Jesus tells us, "Love your enemies." Many of us find it difficult to get along with our friends, to say nothing of loving our enemies. It all stems from attitude.

You can sit down to a meal and begin to think, *Now I know that's going to taste bad. That's liver and onions—I can't stand liver and onions.* (I kind of feel that way myself.) But I know that if I just sit down there and say, "Now, Mr. Liver and Mrs. Onions, you've been wed, but you don't belong in my stomach," the moment I take a bite, my stomach will rebel, and I'm likely to bring it back—all because of the attitude. But if I sit at the table and say, "Now, liver and onions, there's nothing better. [Lord, forgive me for telling a story!] I just love liver and onions. I can't wait to get at it," it will go down so smoothly, easily. I'll just sit back and relax and enjoy the liver and onions. Do you know why? Because I programmed myself in my attitudes and thoughts to like it.

Learn to like even those things which seem to be unlikable. When your attitude is right, you will be visiting, sharing, witnessing, growing, going and glowing for Christ. "Let this mind be in you, which was also in Christ Jesus."

Can you imagine Jesus Christ complaining, bickering, criticizing, talking about somebody else, bad-mouthing? No. Because He thought right, His words were right. And the same mind in us will produce the same kind of thinking and the same kind of words and the same kinds of actions and deeds.

There is another side to that coin. When your attitude is wrong, everything about you will be wrong. I don't care how right it is, it will seem wrong if your attitude is wrong. Not only that, but you'll feel bad, look bad, talk bad, see bad, do bad; consequently, you'll *be* bad. The wrong attitude will poison your mind, your soul, your heart. It will upset the chemical balance of your body and your metabolism. It will cause you to feel undue pressure and increase your problems, intensify your pain and accent your weaknesses. So have the right attitude. Things that really are bad will seem better if you approach them with the right attitude.

Have the right attitude.

You can hate your job. I mean, it's the worst job in all the world. You can get up on a morning and dread to go to your job, and it will be the worst thing you can encounter. But if you say, "The job is not so bad after all, and it will last only eight or ten hours, and then I'll be through for today; and I will find one thing in my job—one person or one activity—that I really like," you'll be surprised how your job will change. No, your job won't change, but your attitude toward your job will change.

My message is "The Attitude of Superiority." One of the things that the Apostle Paul said in II Timothy, chapter 3, will characterize the last days is people thinking they are more than they really are. He uses the term "highminded." He says that in the last days men shall be high-minded—that is, entertaining, encompassing, embracing a feeling of superiority; thinking themselves a cut above, better than, higher than anybody else. We must guard against that feeling because it causes problems in the innermost being.

Observe with me four things that we must deal with in coping with the attitude of superiority.

Most importantly, you must

I. KNOW YOURSELF

You must know *who* you are, *what* you are, *where* you are and *why* you are. Why this body of clay? Why this stature? Why this mind? Why this soul? Why my particular style or form in life? Why, on this globe of six billion people, is there somebody like me?

As you evaluate yourself, there is one simple, basic, fundamental rule you must follow: Don't think too highly of yourself. If we could buy some people for what they're worth, then sell them for what they think they're worth, we could be instant millionaires. Don't think too highly of yourself.

> Don't think too highly of yourself.

To Romans 12:3, "To every man that is among you, not to think of himself more highly than he ought to think," add I Corinthians 10:12, "Wherefore let him that thinketh he standeth take heed lest he fall"; then II Corinthians 3:5, "Not that we are sufficient of ourselves to think any thing as of ourselves; but our sufficiency is of God"; then Galatians 6:3, "For if a man think himself to be something, when he is nothing, he deceiveth himself."

A lot of people are going around absolutely deceived because they think themselves to be one thing when they are really not that at all. So the basic rule again is, do not think too highly of yourself.

I'm convinced that an honest assessment of our lives will produce two things: (1) it will reveal our strengths, and we all have strong points; (2) it will reveal our weaknesses, and we all have these too.

If the Devil cannot defeat you in your weaknesses, he will try to defeat you in your strengths. In other words, you are on guard when you're weak. You have a barrier up at that point. If the Devil can't get through the barrier and defeat you at a weak point, he'll come at a strong point, catch you off guard and defeat you. Be careful that the Devil can't attack you even in a strong point.

In II Corinthians 12:10 Paul writes, "When I am weak,

then am I strong." Sounds like a paradox, doesn't it? But it isn't. Listen! The weaker Paul felt in his own power and strength, the stronger Christ was to him. That's the way it works. We must admit to our weaknesses in order to draw on the reserve of the strength of Christ. Be careful about your attitude.

Now when you know yourself, you will really know how much you do indeed need God physically, spiritually, emotionally and mentally. You need Him today, tomorrow and for eternity.

Do you really know yourself, or have you been putting up a facade, a front? It's no good to put a big display in a store if you don't have any goods on the shelf. A lot of people—a lot of Christians—are going around with a big front and a big display, but they don't have it on the shelf; and that's hypocrisy. And you know what Jesus thinks of hypocrites. I remind you again of Matthew 22 and 23.

Have you made an honest assessment of your life? Do you know yourself?

II. ACCEPT YOURSELF

In all the wedding ceremonies, there is this little phrase, "for better or for worse."

I heard about the couple who were getting married by a judge. The judge said to her, "Do you take him for better or worse?" She said, "Judge, I don't think he's going to get any better, and God knows he can't get no worse. I'll take him like he is."

You and I must learn to accept ourselves. Some things we cannot change. All too many people are trying a drastic change. Learn to get along with yourself. Just say, *Self, you're all I have, so you and I must agree. Now, Self, we don't like the way our hair grows. I wish it grew like some of these glamour guys; but, Self, get a little can of spray, and do the best you can.*

Do you see what I'm saying? Learn to accept yourself. Isn't it strange that most short people want to be tall and most tall people want to be short. Most thin people want to be fat, and most fat people want to be thin. Most people who have curly hair want it straight, and those with straight hair want it curly. Redheads want to be blonde, or if they have black hair, they want it brown.

> **Learn to accept yourself.**

Folks, if you're short, be proud of every inch. If you're tall, watch out for low ceilings. If you're handsome, be careful. "Mirror, mirror, on the wall, who is the fairest of them all?"—be careful about that. If you are not too good-looking, then welcome to the not-too-good-looking majority in the human race. But be satisfied.

All of us know the name Jimmy Durante, that long-nosed comedian. Durante could just sit around and say, "You know this nose of mine…," and everybody would laugh. It made him millions of dollars. Why? Because Jimmy Durante learned to accept the fact that he had a long nose.

Dr. Louis Entzminger, who also had a long nose, used to say, "The reason my nose is so long, I learned to keep it out of other people's business." That is a good attitude. Mind your own business. If you go around minding somebody else's business, you either don't have a *mind,* or you don't have any *business!*

Jimmy Durante said, "Everybody's got a schnozzle," meaning some kind of defect. Some of you girls have a few freckles, and you're trying your best to do away with them or cover them up. Don't take those freckles off! Some guy somewhere dearly loves freckles. Put a little cream on them, display them, play them up. Make the best of everything. If you have a wart on your nose, make it a good-looking wart. Put a little good-smelling stuff on it. Make the best of any defect. Have a good attitude toward it. There may be a premium on those things someday. In other words, make the most of a handicap or a defect. Major on it. Capitalize on it!

We Christians make up the body of Christ. Now, every person can't be the same member of that body. Paul says in I Corinthians, chapter 12, that we're all members of the same body, but we don't all have the same function. If the eye were an ear, where would be the seeing? Or if the ear were a nose, where would be the hearing? In other words, if we were all ears or all eyes or all nose, wouldn't we look strange? It takes every member—the ear, the eye, the nose, the hand, the foot—it takes the whole composition to make the body. Every member adds to, completes, the body.

And so it is in the body of Christ. Every individual member makes up the body of Jesus Christ. You can't have the same position or the same function as some other member, but be satisfied with the position that you do have and the function that is yours. Learn to accept yourself.

III. ACKNOWLEDGE THE GIFT

Acknowledge that whatever you have is a gift from God. Don't go around boasting about what you have or what you've done or who you are. Acknowledge that whatever gift you have is indeed a gift from God. Again I refer to I Corinthians, chapter 12, where Paul describes the individuality of the members of the body. He says God has given to different ones various gifts. Let me illustrate.

Unless you have a gift for music, you can practice all the days of your life and never become a Paderewski. Now if you don't have that gift, stir up the gift that *is* in you. Do what you can do, and you can be an accomplished person in that field, whatever field it might be. Use that gift. God made you as you are for a purpose.

There are no two individuals alike. There is technically no such thing as "identical" twins. There is no such thing as two snowflakes or two leaves or two trees being alike. There is no exact replica of any person. No two people have the same identity. Nobody's fingerprints are like anyone else's. You are different, even in your fingerprint.

Do you see what I'm saying? That's another attitude. God made you to serve Him. God made you with certain talents. So with all this in mind, thank Him for what He has given you and for the way He has made you. And if you use what you *have*, God will give you what you *need*.

IV. USE WHAT YOU HAVE TO THE GLORY OF GOD

First, know yourself; second, accept yourself; third, acknowledge that all you have is a gift from God; now fourth, use what you have to the glory of God.

In Matthew 5:16 Jesus said, "Let your light so shine before men, that they may see your good works, and glorify your Father which is in heaven." The number one purpose of your life and mine is to glorify Him. If it is with a handicap, use the handicap. If it is with a fully developed mind, body, soul and spirit, use them for Him. Where much is given, much is required.

We read in I Corinthians 10:31, "Whether therefore ye eat, or drink, or whatsoever ye do, do all to the glory of God." And then Colossians 3:17 says, "And whatsoever ye do in word or deed, do all in the name of the Lord Jesus, giving thanks to God and the Father by him." When we reckon with the fact that here we are, individuals made by God, made for His glory, made to serve Him, made as we are by His own choosing, then we have very little to complain about, to be unhappy or conceited about.

There is no room for a superior attitude. Paul says, 'In this flesh there dwelleth no good thing.' At our best we are bad, very bad. At our strongest we are weak, very weak. At our wisest we are unwise, very unwise. So our prayer ought to be, "Lord, here I am. I am Yours. I am ready to go where You want me to go, ready to do what You want me to do, ready to say what You want me to say. My eyes are Yours to see through. My lips are Yours to speak through. My ears are Yours to hear through. My hands are Yours to work with. My feet are Yours to walk with. My body is Your temple. O Lord, take me, mold me, make me, use me. This is my prayer."

> There is no room for a superior attitude.

At a missions conference a man with one leg hobbled to the front on crutches. As he came down the aisle struggling with his crutches, all eyes were on him. The preacher had called for somebody to surrender for the foreign field. Nobody answered that call except this one-legged man.

After the singing had finished, the pastor said to him, "Dear brother, with all these people out here with two legs, tell me why you with one leg are the only one to surrender to be a missionary." His answer was simply, "Because, Pastor, I didn't see anybody with two legs surrendering."

Ladies and gentlemen, we should be ready, willing, dedicated, committed to Christ as we are, in an attitude of humility, saying to God, "I'm nothing, but I will do what You ask me to do."

CONCLUSION: You are what you are by the grace of God, and you can become what God wants you to be by committing everything you are into the hands of Jesus Christ.

2.
ATTITUDE OF INFERIORITY

Our primary verse for our entire series is Proverbs 23:7:

"For as he thinketh in his heart, so is he."

My text for this chapter is Numbers 13:33:

"And there we saw the giants, the sons of Anak, which come of the giants: and we were in our own sight as grasshoppers, and so we were in their sight."

Don't look now, but your attitude is showing.

The mind is a wonderful machine—over thirteen billion cells in the average brain. What a capacity—and most of it is going unused! Psychologists tell us that we use only about ten percent of our innate ability.

Did you ever feel like a grasshopper—as though you were unimportant, unneeded, unnecessary, low-down, useless, inadequate, inferior, frustrated, afraid, like a zero with the rim taken off?

Look again at verse 33: "And we were in our own sight as grasshoppers, and so we were in their sight." That text says that when you feel like a grasshopper, you look like a grasshopper to others.

You know the story of the twelve spies sent to spy out the land of Canaan. Ten of these spies had terrible inferiority complexes. They were absolutely positive that they would be defeated. They thought defeat, majored on defeat in their thinking and, in so doing, set the stage for it. By the power of their minds, they preprogrammed themselves for defeat.

There are many defeatists in the world today. They are not satisfied in being defeated themselves only; they want to defeat everybody else also. Some people are defeatists in every area of their lives. Nothing is right, nothing is successful, nothing is triumphant, nothing is victorious; everything is down, everything is bad.

> Attitude governs action, and outlook determines the outcome.

Well, attitude governs action, and outlook determines the outcome. Someone said, "Change your thoughts, and you will change your world." The Bible says, "As he thinketh in his heart, so is he."

Why did these ten, apparently strong, intelligent, productive men, feel so inadequate, so inferior? Why did they feel like grasshoppers in the sight of the giants in the land of Canaan? Simply because they trusted in themselves. Later on in Israel's history, more spies were sent out by Joshua, and they were opposite from these in our text. They were certain of victory because they trusted in God. The bottom line is: we must replace *self-confidence* with *God-confidence*.

The first three verses of Psalm 27 ought to settle a lot of things about **God-confidence.**

"The LORD is my light and my salvation; whom shall I fear? The LORD is the strength of my life; of whom shall I be afraid?

"When the wicked, even mine enemies and my foes, came upon me to eat up my flesh, they stumbled and fell.

"Though an host should encamp against me, my heart shall not fear: though war should rise against me, in this will I be confident."

Confident that God is my helper, that He is for me; and "if God be for us, who can be against us?" We can be sure of the *victory* because we are certain of the *Victor.* Jesus Christ is not a victim, but a victor. He has won the victory, and by faith we appropriate in our personal lives all the victories that Christ has won for us.

One of the most classic examples of an inferiority complex in all the Bible is Moses. You remember that story about Moses in Exodus, chapter 3. The Lord told him, "Moses, I've a job for you to do. Deliver My people."

Moses said, "I-I-I-I c-c-c-can't talk. I've a speech problem."

God said, "Reach over and pick up that snake."

Moses said, "I-I-I-I-I—what d-d-did You s-s-say, Lord?" (Moses not only had a speech problem, but he had a hearing problem!) "Me? Pick up a snake?"

God said to Moses, "I've got a job for you to do." Moses answered God in verse 11: "And Moses said unto God, Who am I...?"

A lot of you have said, when asked to teach a class or drive a bus or work in the children's worship, "Who am I?" Folks, it doesn't matter who *you* are. The important thing comes in verse 14: "God said unto Moses, I AM...." The important thing is not, Who am *I?* The important thing is, God is I AM—"I AM THAT I AM."

He is sufficient for every need, and if we get that into our hearts, we'll know that God can and will do all that He has called and commissioned us to do. He will do it through us.

I get the feeling Moses was sort of hiding behind what we might call an inferiority complex. Maybe he was using that as an excuse not to do what God wanted him to do.

Question: Are you using your inadequacies, your so-called inabilities or handicaps, as excuses? Are you hiding behind something? After all, if it's a speech problem, who made your mouth? God knew that Moses stuttered a bit. I would rather have a person who stutters teaching me the Word of God than one who can speak eloquently trying to teach me something contrary to the Word of God. Don't hide behind an inferiority complex. Moses overcame his inferior feeling when he discovered who God was.

When you and I discover the sufficiency of God and how great, how good, how powerful, how wise, how strong, how sufficient God is, we'll say, "Here I am, Lord. Speak through this stammering tongue. I'll do and say what You want me to do and say. Here I am, Lord. I'm superior in that I have You on my side, and You and I together make a majority."

I. BASIC REASONS FOR INFERIORITY

First of all, let us consider three basic reasons for inferiority.

1. **An unfortunate experience of failure.** Because you failed in one area, you think you will fail in the total scope of your life. But failure is not final. Failure is a part of life, a part of learning.

Look at Thomas A. Edison. Hundreds of times Edison failed in the perfection of the light bulb. If he had quit, we might be sitting around in the dark. Just because he failed did not mean he became overcome by a feeling of inferiority and quit trying.

You can always tell a failure by the way he criticizes a success. Listen! Big men doing big things make big mistakes. Little men doing little things make little mistakes. Some men don't make any mistakes; they don't do anything either.

There is not one single person who has ever accomplished any great feat in life who has not first of all tasted the bitter cup of failure. Don't let failure make you an inferior person. Don't park by your failures. Some people are sitting at the parking meter called Failure, feeding it nickels all day long. They have parked right there by their failure and given up—quit.

A winner never quits, and a quitter never wins. Don't give up. The real man uses his failure as a stepping-stone rather than a stumbling block, and he reaches something higher, bigger and better for Christ.

> Don't park by your failures.

2. **An inadequate assessment of one's ability.** You never help yourself by emphasizing what you cannot do. You will never get anywhere if you sit around and say, "I can't do it." "I can't" never built a class, never built a bus route, never built a church, never accomplished anything. The poet said:

> If you would have some worthwhile plans,
> You've got to watch your *can't*s and *can*s.
> You can't aim low and then rise high;
> You can't succeed if you do not try.

How many people say, "Well, I just can't"? Brother, get you a "*can* opener" and say with Paul, "I can do all things through Christ which strengtheneth me."

3. **A lack of motivation due to a limited faith.** The only thing on earth that can limit God is your unbelief. Your lack of faith will always limit God.

Jesus said in Matthew 17:20, "If ye have faith as a grain of mustard seed, ye shall say unto this mountain, Remove hence to yonder place; and it shall

> Your lack of faith will always limit God.

remove." Where is your faith? "According to your faith be it unto you." Jesus said, "Have faith in God."

Now we ought to have faith in self, but the difference between the humanist and the Christian is, the humanist has faith only in man, and the Christian has faith in God.

II. HOW TO OVERCOME INFERIORITY

How can we overcome inferiority?

1. Acknowledge the unlimited resources of God. God owns everything by virtue of the fact that He created everything. John 1:3 says, "All things were made by him; and without him was not any thing made that was made." God has all power in both worlds. In Matthew 28:18 Jesus said, "All power is given unto me in heaven and in earth."

Now watch this. When a man permits Christ to take the reins of his life, he has all the power of Christ at his disposal. The power of Christ is equal to the power of God, and God's power is always unlimited, always sufficient. Whatever a man can do without Christ, he can do infinitely better with Christ. For you see, Jesus Christ makes new men. Jesus quickens men. He energizes men. He gives men a regenerated power. He equips men to live life to the fullest. Christ qualifies us to face any situation that life demands and brings us out of that situation bigger and better people.

So, to overcome the inferiority complex, acknowledge the resources of God. They are unlimited.

2. Avail yourself of all that God has put at your disposal. Many of us are just nibbling at the crumbs, when we could be taking in all that God has. The supply house of God is full and running over. He has put it at your disposal. Avail yourself of all God has put there. He has placed before you a formula for getting whatever you need. Jesus said in Matthew 21:22, "Whatsoever ye shall ask in prayer, believing, ye shall receive."

He has promised His Spirit to you just for the asking. "If ye then, being evil, know how to give good gifts unto your children: how much more shall your heavenly Father give the Holy Spirit to them that ask him?" (Luke 11:13).

God has promised you the power, the energy of the Holy Spirit to help you overcome those fears, those frustrations, those inadequacies, those limitations, those inferior feelings. Can you imagine anybody who has the Holy Spirit within having any reason to be inferior? The Holy Spirit equips us with all we need.

First, God gives the formula for everything you need. Then He gives the Holy Spirit to energize, to give you power and strength. Then He has promised all the wisdom you need. Not to know what to do with what God has given can be frustrating. But in James 1:5 God has promised wisdom to know how to use what He gives you: "If any of you lack wisdom, let him ask of God, that giveth to all men liberally, and upbraideth not; and it shall be given him."

Isn't God good! He not only says, "Here is the vast storehouse"; He not only says, "Here is My Spirit"; but He says, "Here is the wisdom that you need in order to use properly that with which I entrust you." Avail yourself of all that God has placed at your disposal.

3. **Aspire to develop your God-given potential to its fullest extent.** Why should we be satisfied to have just a part of what God intended us to have or just to be partially what God intended us to be? God intends us to develop physically into mature bodies. He also expects us and wants us to develop spiritually into full-grown, spiritual people and to be mentally mature. Spiritual health, mental health and physical health go together. God wants us to develop to the fullest extent our God-given potential.

It is a shame, a sin, for men and women to waste the potential God has given them. How many today are wasting the greater part of the potential God has placed in them? God has endowed every member of Adam's race with a certain potential, and He enables each one to reach whatever potential He has given him. The tragedy is, in the school of learning, far too many are satisfied with a C on their report cards, when they could be making an A. I'm talking about the school of life and in it the level of accomplishment for Christ, the level of development for Christ and good and righteousness. Why should we settle for an average record and an average grade when we could be at the head of the class with an A+ in the potential God has given us?

Don't be satisfied with God's second best. Don't be satisfied to get just this high or that far when you could go to the very top of the ladder.

One hundred percent of those who succeed in developing their potential may say, "I did." Of those who say, "I will," ninety percent succeed in developing their potential; of those who say, "I can," eighty percent; of those who say, "I think I can," seventy percent; of those who say, "I might," sixty percent; of those who say, "I think I might," fifty percent; of those who say, "What is it?" forty percent; of those who say, "I wish I could," thirty percent; of those who say, "I don't know how," twenty percent; and of those who say, "I can't," only ten percent succeed in developing their potential.

You CAN! You can develop to the fullest extent, to the fullest degree, all the potential God has placed in you. Don't be satisfied with anything less. The greatest danger for most of us is not that we are aiming too high and missing it but that we are aiming too low and reaching it.

The thought, perhaps, that some of you might have is, "Pastor, you've talked about how to overcome this feeling of inferiority; you've spoken of developing the full, God-given potential; now tell me how I can develop that full, God-given potential in my life."

Three simple ways:

Know God personally.

1. **Know God personally.** In Psalm 23:1 the psalmist said, "The LORD is my shepherd [notice the personal emphasis]; I shall not want." If God is the Shepherd and you are the sheep, you don't have to want for anything. All He has, He wants to make available to you.

2. **Trust God implicitly.** Proverbs 3:5,6: "Trust in the

LORD with all thine heart; and lean not unto thine own understanding. In all thy ways acknowledge him, and he shall direct thy paths."

> **Trust God implicitly.**

3. **Cooperate with Him completely.** In John 15:7 Jesus said that if you cooperate with Him and He cooperates with you, whatever you ask will be done for you. Here is how He said it: "If ye abide in me, and my words abide in you, ye shall ask what ye will, and it shall be done unto you." That is cooperating completely, totally, unreservedly with God.

> **Cooperate with Him completely.**

Too many of us are living by the slot machine philosophy. We are feeding life nickels and expecting thousand-dollar bills. We must learn that life is good business, not a gamble. Life is like a mirror: it never gives back more than is put into it. The poet put it this way:

> I've bargained with Life for a penny,
>   And Life would pay no more
> However I begged that evening
>   When I counted my scanty score.
> For Life is a just employer
>   Who gives you what you ask;
> But once you've set the wage,
>   Then you must bear the task.
> I worked for Life for a menial hire,
>   Only to learn, dismayed,
> That all that I'd asked of Life,
>   Life would have paid.

Question: What kind of bargain have you made with life? How much of your potential have you developed? Where are you on the scale of one to ten in the development of the potential that God has given you?

Where much is known, much is required. The more God has given you, the more God has entrusted you with, the greater is your responsibility to Him.

Where are you on the scale of developing the full potential God has placed in you? God has trusted you with the most precious thing in all the earth: L-I-F-E. Some speak so glibly about life, so carelessly, so loosely. Life is an extension of God in a bodily form. God created man, breathed into his nostrils the breath of life, and man became a living soul. Because we are made in the likeness and image of God, He has every right to expect the very best from us.

Where are you? What kind of bargain have you made with life?

CONCLUSION: Whatever your feelings of inadequacy or limitation, *believe* that you can, and with God's help, you can!

3.
ATTITUDE OF PRIDE

I go back again to Proverbs 23:7: "For as he thinketh in his heart, so is he." Change your thoughts, and you change a world. You are not what you think you are, but what you *think,* you *are.*

In Matthew 23:12 our Lord Jesus makes a principle unmistakably clear: "And whosoever shall exalt himself shall be abased; and he that shall humble himself shall be exalted." Whoever exalts himself will be brought low, abased, brought down, humbled; but whoever humbles himself shall be exalted.

The most sinful attitude possessed by men or angels is pride. Our Lord condemned pride more than He did adultery, lying, cheating or stealing. Pride is very insidious. Pride has a tendency to slip into the hearts and lives of even those who are most religious.

Nobody was more religious than the Pharisees. They kept all the Law of Moses. Besides that, they kept six hundred unwritten oral laws; yet the proudest group in Jesus' day were the Pharisees. They thought that they were a cut above everybody else. Look it up. Jesus gives the example of the Pharisee and the publican who went into the temple to pray. The Pharisee lifted up his eyes toward Heaven, made sure he had everybody looking at him and listening to him, then said, 'Lord, I fast. I give tithes.' So what? To tithe is just obeying God's command, and shame on you if you don't! Looking down his nose, the Pharisee said, 'I thank Thee that I am not like this sinner.'

Then the publican, not so much as even lifting his eyes toward Heaven, but smiting upon his breast, cried out, "God be merciful to me a sinner." That's the kind of spirit God honors, acknowledges, recognizes and accepts.

People are proud in different ways of different things. Some, would you believe, are proud of their *humility*. Some are proud of their *ignorance*. Some are proud of their *sweet disposition*. A warning: many a honeybee has drowned in his own honey.

Mr. Spurgeon said—and I think this is good advice— "Be not proud of race, face, place or grace." We have nothing to boast of. All we have is from God—all knowledge, all wisdom, all material possessions, life, breath, strength, health, the earth, the air, the energy, the time. We have nothing to boast of within ourselves.

Someone has observed, and certainly common sense tells us this, that God never intended us to pat ourselves on the back. If He had, He would have made our hinges a bit different. Don't break your arm patting yourself on the back.

Pride! The very first sin on record is related to pride. In Isaiah 14:13,14, Satan said, "I will exalt my throne above the stars of God....I will be like the most High." He was as an angelic being and very religious. In fact, as Lucifer, son of the morning, he was in charge of all worship in Heaven. He was very religious; but when pride swelled up in his heart, he said, 'I'm not satisfied to be on this level. I will exalt my throne above the throne of God. I will be like the Most High. I will be a somebody.'

The moment we say, "*I* will," we follow the example of Satan. On the other side of that coin, at the other end of the spectrum, our Lord in the garden prayed, "*Thy* will...." When we say, "Thy will," we're following the example of Christ.

Let me repeat: The first sin that ever happened in the universe, the first sin that was committed by mankind, was related to pride.

In Genesis 2 the Lord God said to Adam, "Of the tree of the knowledge of good and evil, thou shalt not eat." In other words, "You can't touch this particular thing." No matter what it was, it was God's command that they not eat of it.

But the Devil came along. In his dirtiest deal, he said to Eve:

"Yea, hath God said, Ye shall not eat of every tree of the garden?...Ye shall not surely die: For God doth know that in the day ye eat thereof, then your eyes shall be opened, and ye shall be as gods, knowing good and evil."—Gen. 3:1–5.

Think for a moment. The human concept of things is to be more and better and higher and bigger; and who would not want to be like God? So pride entered the heart of the first parents; and through pride, they disobeyed God, listened to Satan; and the first sin—partaking of the forbidden fruit—was committed in the Garden of Eden.

Pride is a heart matter. In Mark 7:21–23, our Lord says:

"For from within, out of the heart of men, proceed evil thoughts, adulteries, fornications, murders,

"Thefts, covetousness, wickedness, deceit, lasciviousness, an evil eye, blasphemy, pride, foolishness:

"All these evil things come from within, and defile the man."

Pride has its roots in this world system. In I John 2:15 and 16 it is written:

"Love not the world, neither the things that are in the world. If any man love the world [this world system in which we live], *the love of the Father is not in him.*

"For all that is in the world, the lust of the

> Pride is anti-God and anti-Christian.

flesh, and the lust of the eyes, and the pride of life, is not of the Father, but is of the world."

Pride has its roots in this world system. Pride is anti-God, anti-Christ and anti-Christian. If someone were to ask you, "What is the one sin that keeps more people out of Heaven than any other thing? adultery? drunkenness? lying? cheating? stealing?" you should answer, "None of these. The answer is pride."

In Matthew 18:3 Jesus said, "Except ye be converted, and become as little children, ye shall not enter into the kingdom of heaven." The reason some people are not saved is that they are so proud; therefore, they are not willing to humble themselves before God. They are not willing to become as little children, dependent totally, completely upon God. Pride keeps people from the altar, and pride will keep many out of Heaven. They are too proud to kneel before the cross, to kneel before Jesus Christ and to cry out for mercy. Thinking themselves self-sufficient, they are not willing to humble themselves before God in order to be saved.

How easy, then, to see that pride is our worst enemy. It robs us of our friends, separates husbands and wives, drives a wedge between business partners and associates. Pride deprives men of some of life's greatest gifts. How many times have we heard, "Well, I'm a self-made man." Everybody who has gotten anywhere has gotten there by the help of others but, primarily and foremost, by the help of God.

The worst thing about pride is that it rules God out of the game. If a man could be self-made, the first thing he would do is fall in love with his maker. Did you get that? If a man could make himself, if he could be self-made, he would fall in love with his maker. And any man in love with himself doesn't have much competition nor many rivals. A man wrapped up in himself makes a mighty small package.

I. HOW DOES PRIDE AFFECT PEOPLE?

First, pride leads people to think more highly of themselves than they ought to think. Such an attitude is contrary to Scripture. Romans 12:3 warns, 'Let no man think more highly of himself than he ought to think.' One who thinks too highly of himself is commonly known as an egotist. Someone said an egotist is that conceited dolt who thinks he knows as much as you do. Someone said that an egotist is someone who likes mirrors but never can understand what other people see in them. Someone said an egotist is an "I" specialist. (What do you have when two egotists meet? A perfect case of an "I" for an "I.") The best definition is this one I picked up somewhere: "Egotism is the hypodermic that God allows a man to administer to himself to deaden the pain of being a fool."

Some folks are kind of like the rooster that I heard about. He thought that the sun rose every morning just to hear him crow!

Most of those inflated with ego are full of hot air. When we think ourselves better than others, we become critical of others. We become jealous of others. We become self-assertive, sarcastic, resentful. The proud person is often aggressive, argumentative and irritable. Pride causes people to think more highly of themselves than they should.

The second thing pride does: it causes strife and contention. Proverbs is the book of wisdom in the Bible, and in chapter 13, verse 10, the wise Solomon gives us a word about contention and pride and their relationship: "Only by pride cometh contention." Pride causes strife. As I said, the proud person is often aggressive, argumentative and irritable. Wise Solomon backs it up by saying, 'Pride brings contention.'

> **Pride causes strife and contention.**

Let's think about contention in the home. When we are

wrong, and we know we are wrong, many of us are so proud that we're not willing to admit to the other person in the home that we are wrong. Why? Simply because we're proud, and pride causes contention.

Deep down in your heart you know that argument you had today was your fault, but you haven't admitted, "Honey, I know it was my fault. I'm going to swallow my pride and admit that I was wrong." That will save a lot of contention in your home. Don't look like angels. What I am saying is not foreign to you, I know.

Pride also causes contention in the church. In the Upper Room in the last few moments of their time with the Lord Jesus, the disciples entered into an argument about who was going to be the greatest. The Bible says that there arose a strife among the disciples, arguing over who was going to sit at a particular place at the table. Pride causes contention, strife, discord, disharmony, disunity, troubles, problems and division even in the church.

Pride causes contention in a nation, in government. In Daniel, chapter 4, a great man, Nebuchadnezzar, believed himself to be king of kings. He built the hanging gardens of Babylon, one of the seven wonders of the world. One day he strolled out on his porch and said, 'I, Nebuchadnezzar, have built all of these wonderful things. This is my glory.' And the Bible says while he was yet speaking, God said to him, "Wait a minute! Because you have not given Me glory, I am going to drive you into the wild, and for seven long years you will live like an animal."

For seven years Nebuchadnezzar crawled around on all fours. And the Bible says his hair grew like eagles' feathers and his nails, like birds' claws. For seven long years he endured that because of one single sin—pride. Nebuchadnezzar thought himself the king of kings, but God says that glory belongs to Him, and He will not let anyone else have it. Nebuchadnezzar was restored back to his sanity when he was willing to say that all power belongs to God.

Pride causes contention and strife. The wise Solomon put it this way, "Pride goeth before destruction, and an haughty spirit before a fall." If you don't believe that, talk to Nebuchadnezzar.

Someone has noted that Hostility is Pride's twin brother. When we become proud, we become hostile, and the one full of pride lacks the love of God. First Corinthians 13:4 states, "Charity [love]…is not puffed up." Love is not proud, so when pride comes in, love is diminished.

I repeat: pride causes people to think more highly of themselves; pride causes strife and contention; and pride leads to *vanity*.

In the prophecy of Isaiah, chapter 3, verse 16 says:

"Moreover the LORD *saith, Because the daughters of Zion* [the women in Israel] *are haughty, and walk with stretched forth necks and wanton eyes, walking and mincing as they go* [pride—look at it], *and making a tinkling with their feet."*

Verse 18 talks of the ornaments about their feet and round tires like the moon and chains and bracelets and mufflers and bonnets and ornaments of the legs, and all the rest.

"And it shall come to pass, that instead of sweet smell there shall be stink; and instead of a girdle a rent; instead of well set hair baldness; and instead of a stomacher a girding of sackcloth; and burning instead of beauty."—Vs. 24.

Pride leads to vanity. And, men, we're about as bad as the women.

| Pride leads to vanity. |

We were down at a little cottage on the lake, and the electricity went out. Man, I almost had a "fit"! I couldn't blow my hair dry! I like to do that; it makes me look better! We ought not to be so proud that we are led into vanity and the Lord has to bring us down from that high seat of vanity and vain living.

II. WHAT DOES GOD THINK ABOUT PRIDE?

God looks at pride two ways. First, He hates pride. Out of the book of Proverbs come many wonderful jewels of wisdom. How does God feel about pride?

"These six things doth the LORD hate: yea, seven are an abomination unto him:

"A proud look, a lying tongue [He groups pride with all these cardinal sins], *and hands that shed innocent blood,*

"An heart that deviseth wicked imaginations, feet that be swift in running to mischief,

"A false witness that speaketh lies, and he that soweth discord among brethren."—Prov. 6:16–19.

Pride is the first thing on the list of the seven things God hates.

Not only that, but God resists anything that has to do with pride. James 4:6 says, "Wherefore he saith, God resisteth the proud." Remember, God *hates* pride, and God *resists* pride. Those are the two ways God looks at this awful sin, and pride is a sin because anything contrary to the law of God and the way of God is sin.

III. WHAT IS THE GREATEST CURE FOR PRIDE?

Man's basic makeup, his basic characteristic, is to be proud; and there is only one antidote—*humility.* Someone asked, "But how can I handle my pride?" The only way is to become humble before God. The only way to be humble is for you to *humble yourself.* Do you remember my text? "He that shall humble himself...."

Now that suggests to me that that is something we must do. It must be a definite and deliberate act of the will. It's not something that's going to come automatically. You can sit around and say, "Now, Lord, make me humble" all you want to, but God is not going to do it that way. The Scripture is plain in saying that you and I must humble ourselves. Not only does my text say it, but James 4:10 says, "Humble yourselves in the sight of the Lord, and he shall lift you up."

I repeat: To humble yourself is an act of your own volition, your own will, your own mind, your own action.

"Likewise, ye younger, submit yourselves unto the elder. Yea, all of you be subject one to another, and be clothed with humility: for God [the second time this is written in the book] *resisteth the proud, and giveth grace to the humble.*

"Humble yourselves therefore under the mighty hand of God [a deliberate act of your own will], *that he may exalt you in due time."*—I Pet. 5:5,6.

How can we handle our pride? By learning to humble ourselves.

In the process of humbling, three things are absolutely necessary:

> **We should learn to humble ourselves.**

1. **Admit that you need God's help.** In John 15:5 Jesus said, "Without me ye can do nothing."

2. **Confess pride as you would any other sin.** Remember, pride is the number one sin that God hates. This sin keeps a lot of people out of Heaven. The first cause and root of all sin was when Satan said, "I will." When man listened to Satan and disobeyed God, it was because of pride. So you and I must confess pride as we would any other sin.

First John 1:9 says, "If we confess our sins, he is faithful and just to forgive us our sins, and to cleanse us from all unrighteousness." Pride is a sin, and all sin must be confessed.

3. **Seek divine guidance.** You and I cannot go long without going wrong. Proverbs 14:12 says, "There is a way which seemeth right unto a man, but the end thereof are the ways of death." Seek divine guidance. In Psalm 32:8, this is what God offers you: "I will instruct thee and teach thee in the way which thou shalt go: I will guide thee with mine eye."

We need divine guidance every day. If we are going to humble ourselves before God, we must admit our need for Him. We must confess pride as a sin. We must seek divine guidance.

Do you really want peace of mind? Would you really like to discover the secret of happiness? There is one way. Blend your will with God's will and yield yourself completely, totally, unreservedly to Him.

Remember now, there are two wills: God's will and your will. As long as these wills are separate, there will be friction. God's will is to go the upward way. Man's will is by nature to go the downward way. So you must blend your will with God's will and yield yourselves completely to Him, and then happiness, peace and joy will be yours.

| Humble your-self before God. |

Someone asked Augustine, one of the early church fathers, "What is the first Christian grace?" He answered, "Humility." "What then is the next?" He answered, "Humility. For," said Augustine, "when you humble yourself, you have all the graces of the Christian faith." How true it is! Humble yourself before God.

CONCLUSION: I bring this to a close with the words of Jesus in Matthew 5:5: "Blessed are the meek: for they shall inherit the earth."

4.
ATTITUDE OF JEALOUSY

"For as he thinketh in his heart, so is he."—Prov. 23:7.

"Set me as a seal upon thine heart, as a seal upon thine arm: for love is strong as death; jealousy is cruel as the grave: the coals thereof are coals of fire, which hath a most vehement flame."—Song of Sol. 8:6.

Jealousy is as cruel as the grave.

Don't look now, but your attitude may be showing.

Webster defines *jealousy* as "a jealous resentment against a person enjoying success or advantage." In everyday language it says this: jealousy is an evil attitude toward another person who has advanced in some measure further than we have.

Dr. J. Frank Norris used to put it this way: "People are jealous of other people for one of three reasons: the other person *knows* more, *has* more or can *do* more." Pick out the object of your jealousy and just think about the thing of which you are jealous in somebody's life; it will be because that person knows more, has more or can do more.

The objects of jealousy are three in number. This covers the entire spectrum of all human relationships: **possessions, position** and **personality**. Again, anybody or anything of which you are jealous would be because of **possessions** that person has, because of the **position** that person has or because of that person's **personality**, and that includes a whole lot. So I'm underscoring and getting to the bottom line of it all: jealousy is an evil attitude toward somebody else because that somebody is in a better position, has more possessions or a more pleasing personality or something that you covet and you envy that you do not have.

Here is something you don't want to forget: "Sticks and stones are thrown at fruit-bearing trees."

> "Sticks and stones are thrown at fruit-bearing trees."

A fellow may be making fifty cents an hour more than you, or he knows more, has more or can do more. That may cause you jealousy.

In researching the definition of *jealousy,* I learned that jealousy and envy are very closely related—perhaps they are first cousins. In fact, Webster's dictionary goes on to say that *jealousy* means "resentfully envious of another person." The first synonym listed for *jealousy* in Webster is *envy.* So the two are very close kin—jealousy and envy. Jealousy nurtures hostile feelings. Jealousy encourages harmful actions. Jealousy wounds another person just for the sake of wounding him. Jealousy seeks its own. Jealousy is puffed up. To sum it all up, jealousy hurts just for the enjoyment of hurting.

> "Tell me," said the willow to the thorn, "why art thou so envious of the clothes of those who pass by? Of what use can they be to thee?"
>
> "None whatsoever," replied the thorn. "I have no desire to wear them. I only want to tear them."

That's jealousy—that's envy: seeking harm just for the sheer delight of it. No wonder the Bible describes envy as being devilish. First John 3:12 says, "Not as Cain, who was of that wicked one [the Devil], and slew his brother. And wherefore slew he him? Because his own works were evil, and his brother's righteous." I cite that verse to underscore that the Bible describes envy and jealousy as being devilish.

Did you know that envy (jealousy) is described as the work of the flesh? Open your Bible to Galatians 5:19–21: "Now the works of the flesh are manifest, which are these...." In these verses adultery, fornication, lasciviousness, witchcraft, idolatry, murder, drunkenness, etc., are listed in the same category as jealousy.

You may say, "Well, my sin is not so bad." Who said? Envy (jealousy) is listed with murder and adultery. An evil, resentful, envious feeling toward another person is a sin in God's sight.

Paul lists envy in another place with the grosser sins of life:

"Being filled with all unrighteousness, fornication, wickedness, covetousness, maliciousness; full of envy, murder, debate, deceit, malignity; whisperers,

"Backbiters, haters of God, despiteful, proud, boasters, inventors of evil things, disobedient to parents."—Rom. 1:29,30.

Envy (jealousy) is listed among the baser, grosser sins committed by the human family. Jealousy is a universal disease. It is prevalent among both Christians and non-Christians. It strikes the rich and the poor, the learned and the unlearned, the educated and the uneducated, the small and the great, the good and the bad, the tall and the short, the skinny and the fat—everybody, everywhere.

Say, when you feel yourself turning green with jealousy, it means you are ripe for trouble. Be careful; your attitude may be showing.

Jealousy is even in the animal world. Let me cite you a couple of examples.

My wife and I were visiting with the Erwin family last week. They have a big dog and a little dog. The big dog is very big, and the little dog is very little. The big dog is named Wolfe—and he looks like one; the little dog is named Slugger—and he looks like anything but a slugger. While we were there, through the den windows and out on the patio, Wolfe showed up. Little Slugger barked and barked.

He was ready to tear the place up. They told us when they take the dogs to the veterinarian, they have to take them in two cars, because little Slugger is so jealous of big Wolfe— in the animal kingdom, mind you.

In my office this week, there were two flies. I felt something biting me on the ankle. I just thought it was another one of those whatever it is I have! I didn't know flies could bite like that. I had no idea it was a fly. So I just ignored it for a few minutes. Then it got to stinging so badly, I looked down, and lo and behold, there was a fly on my ankle biting me through my sock. Another one flew up, and that one flew off. They were taking turns! They were jealous of the sweet-tasting blood.

I. WHERE IS JEALOUSY FOUND?

The first place is within family circles.

In Genesis 37:3, 4, 11:

"Now Israel [Jacob] *loved Joseph more than all his children."* Why? He was the baby. Have you noticed that when several years have passed and a baby is born, the older children get just a bit jealous of the teensy-weensy, itsy-bitsy little baby? The same thing happened here. Joseph was loved of his father.

Verse 4: *"And when his brethren saw that their father loved him more than all his brethren, they hated him, and could not speak peaceably unto him."*

Now verse 11: *"And his brethren envied him...,"* or were jealous of him. You know the story, how they tried to destroy their brother Joseph because they were so envious and jealous of his having the love and affection of their father.

Jealousy is not confined to the ancient past and the patriarchal families. Jealousy raises its ugly head in modern families too, in Fort Worth and Arlington and Grand Prairie and Dallas and all over Texas and all over the United States. Parents may show affection for one child for some particular reason, and all the other children get jealous. One family member has more success in the business world, and the other family members get jealous. In a Will, heirs are named or not named, and there is a lot of jealousy and fighting and fussing and bickering because one is jealous of another.

At family reunions, did you ever notice that the little fair-haired boy always gets the attention and admiration of all the kissing cousins that haven't seen him for a long time, causing the others to get just a bit jealous? Jealousy shows up in the family.

The second place where jealousy is found is in public life. Turn to I Samuel, chapter 18. In the life of the government of the kings is a perfect and classic example of jealousy.

"And David went out whithersoever Saul sent him, and behaved himself wisely: and Saul set him over the men of war, and he was accepted in the sight of all the people, and also in the sight of Saul's servants.

"And it came to pass as they came, when David was returned from the slaughter of the Philistine, that the women came out of all cities of Israel, singing and dancing, to meet king Saul, with tabrets, with joy, and with instruments of music.

"And the women answered one another as they played, and said, Saul hath slain his thousands, and David his ten thousands.

"And Saul was very wroth, and the saying displeased him; and he said, They have ascribed unto David ten thousands, and to me they have ascribed but thousands: and what can he have more but the kingdom?

"And Saul eyed David from that day and forward."—Vss. 5–9.

David got the applause. "Saul hath slain his thousands, and David his ten thousands." Suddenly the old green-eyed monster began to swell up in Saul, and from then on he designed in his heart to destroy David.

Jealousy wants to destroy its object. But wait! Jealousy always destroys the one who has it in his heart as well as sometimes the object of it. Human experience will tell you that.

> Jealousy wants to destroy its object.

What about the popular girl in high school who gets the first date with a new boy in town? Uh-huh. All the other girls are green with envy. What about the athletic young man who gets the scholarship and the attention of the cheerleaders? All the other teammates get a bit jealous. What about the neighbor who gets a new car? Someone said nothing depreciates an old car faster than having a neighbor get a new one!

What about the clerk who is always making the biggest sale? The other clerks get a bit jealous because the manager comes around and says, "Man! You are doing a good job! Here's a reward." Well, if you want to get the manager's praise, don't stand there like somebody who doesn't know where he is. Get busy! Earn it! What about the employee who gets the biggest merit raise? What about ten thousand other things that people get jealous about?

After a man makes his mark in the world, a multitude come running with erasers. Some people can't stand for other people to have progress and success and advantage. This eats on them until it shows up all over them. Let somebody get a new suit or a new house or a new car, and these jealous, green-eyed monsters rise up in these so-called quiet, peaceful people who inside are bitter, resentful and envious. And that is a sin before God.

The third place where jealousy is found is within church memberships. This is most tragic of all. There is no wrath like religious wrath. The very first murder in history was the result of a worship and religious service. Cain and Abel went to worship. Cain brought his offering. Abel brought his.

Abel's offering was of the flock, not of his own hand. Cain brought that of his own doings. God looked upon Abel's offering and accepted it. He looked upon Cain's offering and rejected it. Immediately strife (jealousy) rose up in Cain. And the Bible says he slew his brother because he was envious. That's religious jealousy.

A few years ago I was called to be the mediator in a church fight. I have never been in a church fight, and I hope I never get in one. What causes church fights? Jealousy, envy, immaturity on the part of Christians. But I was called to mediate, referee, or whatever.

My wife and I arrived on the scene. It was summertime, but I felt a north wind you wouldn't believe! You talk about a blue norther coming down in the summer. Brother, it came down!

When we went into the church, there sat a little group over here, and there sat a little group over there. There was a whole section between them. Four or five of the former pastors were there. A certain crowd in that church had run off every pastor they had ever had. The one there then had been there longer than any other pastor, and the church was thirty-five or forty years old.

Well, the pastor introduced me. I called on the leadership of this faction over here, the pastor's friends. They had their say. Then over here sat the people who were against the pastor. I mean, one guy was angry. I said, "Now, dear brother [I don't know whether I should have called him a brother, because one in that spirit is not very brotherly], just what do you want to do to this pastor?" He balled up his fist and said, "I want to pop him right on the nose."

I said, "Brother, if that's the spirit of Christ, go ahead and do it." He sat down. But a few days later, a group of that crowd found the pastor downtown and mobbed him and beat him up. Now this was in the twentieth century.

Religious wrath is a terrible thing. Jealousy in a church is despicable and despisable. It grieves the Holy Spirit of God.

Someone gets a certain class to teach, and others get jealous. Someone gets more attention from the Sunday school superintendent. Someone gets the solo part in the music. Someone gets elected to a certain office. Someone apparently gets more attention from the pulpit. All this causes jealousy among some. Of all places that jealousy should not be is the house of God, among the family of God.

II. WHAT DOES JEALOUSY DO?

Jealousy does three things primarily:

First, it separates one from other people. Paul says, 'Why are there bitterness and envy and division and strife among you? You are divided' (I Cor. 3:3). He is talking to the church at Corinth. Jealousy divides; it separates one from another.

> **Jealousy separates one from other people.**

Second, it separates one from God. When Jesus was brought by the chief priest before Pilate, we read, 'And Pilate knew that it was because of envy [jealousy] that they had brought Jesus before him' (Mark 15:10). Pilate discerned that the Jews were jealous of Jesus Christ, and their jealousy separated them from God in the flesh in the Person of His Son, Jesus Christ. Jealousy separates a person from God.

> **Jealousy separates one from God.**

Third, jealousy becomes the master of one's life. Like a Frankenstein, it returns to haunt the attacker more than the attacked. I said a bit ago that usually jealousy does more harm to the person who has it inside than to the object of his or her jealousy. Jealousy destroys the person who is jealous.

Being overcome with jealousy is like running into the ocean: the deeper you get in, the harder it is to get out. Shakespeare says in *Othello*, "O, beware, my lord, of jealousy: It is the green-eyed monster which doth mock the meat it feeds on."

> **Jealousy becomes the master of one's life.**

A classic example of jealousy destroying the one who harbors it is found in Esther 7:10: "They hanged Haman on the gallows that he had prepared for Mordecai." I don't have time to review the whole story, but you know how Haman plotted to destroy the Jews and Mordecai. Here is the story: Haman was invited to a great banquet. He was just feeling so up-and-up about it until he got near the king's door and saw old Mordecai. He went back and said to his wife, "What am I going to do about this fellow Mordecai?" Haman brought all his servants in, and they all agreed on one thing: "He's got to be destroyed. Build a gallows for him and hang him on it." So he built a gallows.

On that same night the king couldn't sleep, and he had one of his servants bring him the annals—the history of his kingdom. He was reading along and found where several years previously, a Jew by the name of Mordecai had turned in to him a plot against his life. He said to his servants, "What did we ever do to reward this man for saving my life?" They said, "You never did anything." He said, "All right, bring Haman in." He said to Haman, "What do you think ought to be done for a fellow who showed a favor to the king?"

Haman thought, *O boy! He's going to do me right now!* So Haman said, "You ought to at least get him one of your old suits and one of your horses, and let's parade him up and down the streets."

The king said, "Go get Mordecai. Give him one of my suits. Put him on my horse and ride him up and down the streets." You see, Haman thought the king was going to do something great for him, but the whole plot backfired in his face. Later, Esther revealed his plot against the Jews, and Haman was found guilty.

The whole scheme of your jealous, envious, resentful attitude will also backfire in your face. The Bible says that Haman was hanged on the gallows built to hang Mordecai on. Like a Frankenstein, jealousy returns to haunt the attacker more than the attacked.

III. HOW CAN ONE BE DELIVERED FROM JEALOUSY?

There are three things you must do in setting yourself free from the awful entrapment and enslavement of jealousy:

1. Like any disease, admit that you have it and seek the very best cure. If in a few days an unusual sore appears somewhere on your face or arm or on another part of your body, immediately you think, *I must go to the doctor and get cured.*

Let me ask you why you wouldn't show the same concern about a disease that is ten times deadlier than cancer? Infection will only spread if you postpone the treatment, saying, "Well, it's not so bad at this stage." That doesn't stop the spreading of a disease. And you can say about your sin of jealousy, "I can control it. I can contain it. It won't spread because it is in its early stages." But it will spread like cancer.

2. After you have admitted it, confess your need of healing to the Great Physician who alone can heal you. Jesus is the Healer of body, soul, mind and spirit. Confess it to Him, because He alone can heal.

First John 1:9 reads, "If we confess our sins [you have already admitted it's a sin; now you are confessing it], he is faithful and just to forgive us our sins, and to cleanse us from all unrighteousness."

3. **Follow the doctor's orders.** You are sick. You go to the doctor. "Well, Doc, I have such and such a problem."

I was having a terrible time with an allergy, so I went to the doctor. I sat waiting for about thirty minutes. Then I sat there another fifteen minutes while he stuck all these ice-cold instruments in my nose and ears. When he got through, he said, "Clinically, I would diagnose that you have an allergy. That will be twenty dollars."

I said, "Thanks, Doc, I already knew it was an allergy." He gave me prescriptions for two different medicines. I wanted to get rid of that allergy, so what did I do? Did I go home and say, "Man! He's got beautiful handwriting! I'm going to tack these up on the wall"? Did I tack up two prescriptions on the wall, look at them for seven days and continue sneezing? You know I didn't do that.

But that is the way some of us are doing. You say, "The Bible is a beautiful Book. I'm going to wrap it up with Grandma's shawl and put it down in the trunk so nothing will happen to it."

You had better let something happen to it! You'd better let it get in your heart and mind and soul, because God's Word is the only prescription that will cure the ills of your life. Take the Medicine. Take the Prescription.

Where is it found? In I Corinthians 13:4: "Love envieth not." Isn't that simple? God just makes things so simple for us. He says in so many words, "Get enough of the love of My Son, Jesus Christ, in your heart, and there will not be any room for envy or jealousy, resentment and ill feeling toward your fellowman." Love looks through a telescope while jealousy looks in a microscope and tries to blow everything out of proportion.

CONCLUSION: Jealousy, like a cancer, eats insidiously at your soul and leaves you the skeleton of a living corpse.

5.
ATTITUDE OF DOUBT

"For as he thinketh in his heart, so is he."—Prov. 23:7.

We have said before, you are not what you think you are, but what you *think,* you *are.* Change a man's thoughts, and you change the world in which he lives. Paul said, "Let this mind be in you, which was also in Christ Jesus."

"Jesus answered and said unto them, Verily I say unto you, If ye have faith, and doubt not, ye shall not only do this which is done to the fig tree, but also if ye shall say unto this mountain, Be thou removed, and be thou cast into the sea; it shall be done.

"And all things, whatsoever ye shall ask in prayer, believing, ye shall receive."—Matt. 21:21,22.

Look at the words "doubt not" and then the word "believing."

Don't look now, but your attitude is showing.

Let me say that doubt restricts every phase of human activity. No man can be at his best as long as there are question marks about the essentials, the important things, and the truths of God's Word. It doesn't matter how much talent he has, how much energy he has, how much education he has, if a man doubts what God has said, or entertains question marks where the truth of God is emphatically stated, he cannot be at his best. So doubt restricts human activity.

> **Doubt restricts human activity.**

I. WHAT DOES DOUBT DO?

I have jotted down seven things that doubt will do:

Doubt questions God.

1. Doubt questions God. It is always wrong; it is always grievous to the Holy Spirit, to doubt or question God. Doubt puts a question mark where God has placed an exclamation point. If God says it, that settles it and we ought to believe it.

The approach, the scheme, the plan, the plot of Satan was to put a question mark where God had made a declarative sentence. God declared that if man disobeyed Him by eating of the forbidden fruit, man would die. But Satan came and said, "Hath God said...?" That put a question where God had put a period. God said it, the Devil questioned it, and consequently our first parents, by listening to and believing the Devil (doubting God is what it amounts to), plunged the whole human race into sin.

2. Doubt lowers one's plane of spiritual living. God wants us to live on a high, productive hallelujah plane.

Doubt lowers one's plane of spiritual living.

Now, I am not saying there aren't some valleys in your Christian experience. Everybody has some valleys. But if you set up housekeeping in a valley, if you drive down your stakes in a valley of doubt and despondency, discouragement and fear, you are going to be reduced to a very low level of spiritual living. It all stems from doubt.

3. Doubt diminishes the level of your accomplishment.

Doubt diminishes the level of your accomplishment.

Nobody accomplishes anything who goes around doubting. You see, doubt always leads to disillusionment and discouragement, and God never uses a discouraged person. God cannot use a discouraged Sunday school teacher or a discouraged bus worker or soul winner or music worker or preacher.

Discouragement is contagious, and doubt is contagious. One fellow says, "Say that again. I've been thinking the same thing." The next fellow says, "Say that again. I've been thinking the same thing." And so it passes on, and everybody gets in that low ebb of spiritual life—discouragement.

Discouragement is a demon, and you have every right to rebuke that demon in the name of Jesus Christ. Don't doubt Him.

4. **Doubt disturbs the status of the economy.** Did you know that? Let me show you what I mean.

For example, if you have a product and you doubt that you are going to sell that product, you start out reducing your income. Now, I'm not a monetary expert or a sales expert, but

> Doubt disturbs the status of the economy.

I have been around the block two or three times. I used to sell vacuum cleaners.

I see some of our students making nine or ten dollars an hour out here on the dock—they never had it so good. I remember when I was in seminary thirty years ago. I made fifty cents for every contact I made selling insurance.

Then I sold vacuum cleaners. I can see myself now getting on a Fort Worth Transit Company bus with a big Electrolux in one hand and a bag of accessories in the other, going out to sell vacuum cleaners.

My product was Electrolux. When I went to the door, I didn't say, "Would you like to buy a nice Hoover? I really don't think the Electrolux will clean. I doubt what they say about it." I certainly didn't doubt that Electrolux was the best vacuum cleaner on the market. I did not doubt that it would do what the Electrolux folks said it would do. Therefore, I did not reduce my status of income. When you are making nothing, you can't reduce it to anything, so there I was.

But doubt absolutely, positively limits and disturbs the economy.

If you come to church and say, "Well, I just sort of doubt whether I can give anything," and you don't put anything in the offering, that lowers the offering. That lowers the economy. (By the way, you haven't given God anything until you have given Him a tenth of everything you have. The tithe, ten percent of your income, belongs to Him, and beyond that, the gifts; so let's don't disturb the status of the economy.)

5. **Doubt discourages others.** It affects and discourages everybody around you. If you are always doubting and fearful of what God's going to do or not

| Doubt discourages others. |

going to do, it will discourage others.

6. **Doubt confuses young converts.** Now if those of you who have been saved for a long time go around doubting what God said and what He promised He would do, you confuse a new convert.

| Doubt confuses young converts. |

Here is a young convert who has been saved just a week, a month, a few weeks or a few months. He listens to what you say and picks up on it, and it confuses him. He thought when he got saved that God was going to make a way for him and supply his needs and see him through. Then you express a doubt, and it confuses that young convert. So don't be guilty of doubt.

7. **Doubt degrades the principles of Jesus Christ.** (This is the core, summation and bottom line.) Christ can do anything. When you doubt, you degrade and limit the capability

| Doubt degrades the principles of Jesus Christ. |

of Christ who lives in you. Paul said, "I can do all things through Christ which strengtheneth me." Your doubts will be settled when you adopt that philosophy, that belief, that attitude, that approach to living and to life and to the Bible and to the principles of Christ. You can be a happy, overcoming, victorious, productive, successful Christian. Otherwise, you will be defeated and live on Defeat Avenue all of your life.

II. HOW CAN WE OVERCOME DOUBT?

Turn to Hebrews, chapter 11. Only one weapon can defeat the demon of doubt, and that weapon is faith in God.

You go to sales meetings, and they pump you up: "You can do it! You can do it! You can do it!" But there is a limit to what you can do in the human mind and body.

But, bless God, there is absolutely no limit to what God can do! Hebrews, chapter 11, is the great chapter on faith. The heroes of faith are all listed there.

To me, the most notable example in this whole chapter is Moses. Let me point out three things about the faith of Moses:

1. Moses' faith was instilled in him from childhood. Look at verse 23: "By faith Moses, when he was born, was hid three months of his parents." Something in the parents of Moses motivated them to hide him from the slaughter of Pharaoh. That something was F-A-I-T-H.

Parents and parents-to-be, instill faith in your children's hearts and minds. You may think it's not doing anything, but this message and all these messages go right into the nursery. I know the young ones in there are doing this and that. They are screaming and doing other things, but something is getting through to them.

Don't depend on the pastor and the Sunday school superintendent and the Sunday school teacher to implant faith in your children. The Word of God says when you get up in the morning, tell them about it. When you walk through the day, tell them about it. When you lie down at night, tell them about it. Instill in them that faith.

I can take you to family after family in this church who, twenty years ago when I became pastor, had babies in the nursery. Now those children have babies in the nursery. I can take you to parents who brought their babies to the cradle roll and the kindergarten, stuck an envelope in their hand and taught them to tithe. Now these people are adults, and they are doing the same thing for their babies. They are instilling the faith of God in their children—in babies. It will work.

I went to Sunday school the first time when I was three weeks old, and I haven't missed three weeks in the last twenty-nine years or more.

> Faith must be instilled in our youth during their childhood.

Faith must be instilled in our youth during their childhood. Teach your children; train your children; discipline your children; give them the Word of God. And the Bible says when they are old, they will not depart from it. Give them the Word of God.

2. **Moses' faith increased with maturity.** We don't remain babes in Christ all of our lives; we grow up.

Look at verse 24: "By faith Moses, when he was come to years…." When he matured, what did he do? He made the right choice. That's what mature faith does. Your faith must increase with your maturity in spiritual things.

3. **Moses' faith involved him in a positive action.** Verse 27: "By faith he forsook Egypt." There was a choice of action.

Christianity is likewise a religion of action. We don't just sit still. As one fellow put it, "God didn't save us to sit down and sit. He saved us to git up and git." It's action, and our faith involves us in positive action for Christ—getting involved, sharing, giving, going, telling.

Now I want to tell you three things about *your* faith:

1. **Faith can enable you to know the unknowable.** Look at Hebrews 11:3: "Through faith we understand that the worlds were framed by the word of God."

That is more than these infidel, atheistic, agnostic, unbelieving professors in some colleges and universities and seminaries know. Take a man from behind the plow, take him from out of a machine shop, take him from out of the cab of a truck and teach him the Word of God. He is smarter than a Ph.D. because by faith he understands that the worlds were framed by the Word of God.

2. **Faith can enable you to see the invisible.** Verse 22: "By faith Joseph, when he died, made mention of the departing of the children of Israel; and gave commandment concerning his bones."

I don't have time to dwell on Genesis 50:24,25, but Joseph said, 'I die. Carry my bones from this strange land back to Israel.' Joseph saw that which was invisible. He knew that one day God would deliver the Israelites from four hundred years of bondage and they would go back to their homeland. So he said, "Take my bones with you." That's seeing the invisible.

I remember that in 1974 from our place on Wilbarger Street, we started looking at property. I came to this property so many times. There wasn't anything out here but a big weed patch. I would come and get right out in the middle of those weeds, look around and say, "The kindergarten department would be right here. The junior department would be right here." I would walk over further and say, "The pulpit will be right here."

People must have thought I was crazy when they drove

by and saw a fellow in a dark suit running around out in the weeds. But I was seeing something. "We'll park this bus right here; the choir will be singing right here; children's worship will be going on right here." I was seeing by the eye of faith, before any buildings were ever built, the invisible.

If you don't see anything, you are spiritually blind. You teachers, if you don't see your class filled, it will never be filled. If you don't see your bus filled, it will never be filled. If you don't see the church filled, it will never be filled. We have to see it by the eye that sees the invisible, the eye of faith.

If you have a financial need, look out there and see God meeting that need. If you have weaknesses, problems and discouragements, by faith see that God is going to help you overcome them, and you will. Faith enables you to see the invisible.

3. **Faith enables you to do the impossible.** Jesus is the greatest Authority in all the world. We read all kinds of books. We read what this man says and what that man says, yet we have the greatest Book in all the world.

> **Faith enables you to do the impossible.**

I said to my class again this morning, and I want to say it to you again tonight: The Bible does not need to be rewritten; it needs to be reread. Get in the Book!

Jesus said in Matthew 17:20, "If ye have faith as a grain of mustard seed, ye shall say unto this mountain, Remove hence to yonder place; and it shall remove; and nothing shall be impossible unto you."

The remaining verses of Hebrews 11 repeat over and over, "by faith," "by faith," "by faith," "by faith." These heroes of the Faith did the impossible because they had faith in God.

Anybody would have said it was an impossibility for an army of men to march around a city and have the walls collapse, but faith enables us to do the impossible.

The skeptics say, "The Red Sea could not have opened." Humanly speaking, it couldn't; but by faith it did open. So did the Jordan River. The walls of Jericho did come down. Men received the blessings of God. Widows received their sons again. The blind received sight. The sick received health. The dead received life—ALL BY FAITH. By faith we can do the impossible.

I suppose the most classic example of a doubter, disbeliever and skeptic in all the Bible is Thomas. When you think about Thomas, right away doubting comes to mind—Thomas, the skeptic; Thomas, the doubter.

I will tell you the reason he doubted. Thomas missed church on Sunday night. On Monday the boys gathered around, and one said to Thomas, "Thomas, you don't know what you missed last night!"

"Oh, just a regular Sunday night service, wasn't it?"

"No, no! We saw the Lord last night!"

"You what?"

"We saw the Lord!"

I can imagine that Thomas sat back and laughed. Most doubters, most skeptics, do that. Tell a skeptic you believe the Word is infallible and inspired, and he will just laugh at you.

Thomas said, "You guys have got to be kidding."

They said, "No, we saw the Lord last night."

Thomas said, "Except I see in his hands the print of the nails, and put my finger into the print of the nails [he got right down to the nitty-gritty], and thrust my hand into his side, I will not believe" (John 20:25).

Eight days later, where do you suppose Thomas was? At church! Again, the same thing happened. Jesus came in while they were gathered there in the evening service, and the first thing He did was to point out Thomas. He said, 'Thomas, come here a minute. Put your fingers in the nail prints [God knows what you are thinking; He knows about those doubts]; and, Thomas, put your hand in My side.'

Thomas did and then exclaimed, "My Lord and my God!"

What a testimony! He testified to the deity of the risen Saviour. When all doubts were removed, he testified to the saving power of Christ and to His being alive. You and I can do the same thing when we get doubts out of the way.

Thomas said, "The boys were right. Jesus is alive!"

Jesus said, 'Thomas, you are one of the most blessed men because you have seen Me and believed; but there are some others who are far more blessed. Blessed are they who have not seen and yet believe' (John 20:29).

He is talking about us. With these eyes we have not seen Him. But as Peter said, "Whom having not seen, ye love; in whom, though now ye see him not, yet believing, ye rejoice with joy unspeakable and full of glory" (I Pet. 1:8).

CONCLUSION: May I quote to you a little poem:

> Doubt sees the obstacles;
> Faith sees the way.
> Doubt sees the darkest night;
> Faith sees the day.
> Doubt dreads to take a step;
> Faith soars on high.
> Doubt questions, "Who believes?"
> Faith answers, "I."

Do you believe?

6.
ATTITUDE OF GREED

"For as he thinketh in his heart, so is he."—Prov. 23:7.

The thoughts that race through our minds eventually become the standard of our behavior and the governor of our beings. In the Gospel according to Luke, chapter 6, verse 38, we read:

"Give, and it shall be given unto you; good measure, pressed down, and shaken together, and running over, shall men give into your bosom. For with the same measure that ye mete withal it shall be measured to you again."

Greed can be defined as an excessive or inordinate desire for the acquisition of things.

You know, we are always bothered about things—things material, things temporal, things that will pass, things that have only an earthly value—when our minds should be turned, as Paul tells us, toward heavenly things: "Let this mind be in you, which was also in Christ Jesus" (Phil. 2:5).

"Set your affection on things above, not on things on the earth" (Col. 3:2). Everything in this world system, all material goods of this world, will pass away. Gold and silver, diamonds, rubies, emeralds, pearls and all the rest of the precious stones will one day fade away; but truth, virtue, faith and hope and what you invest in the world above will last forever.

I. WHAT DOES GREED DO?

First, greed turns a person's thoughts toward himself.

How much time do you spend thinking of self? People whose minds are turned toward themselves could be called "me-first" people. "Me-first" people ask these questions: What will you give *me*? What's in it for *me*? What will it profit *me*? "Me-first" people are opposite to "others-first" people.

"Others-first" people generally ask these questions: What can I do for *others*? How may I help *other* people?

Let me say this as a premise upon which we will build the entire message: You will never find happiness in life if your favorite charity is you. If you can't see beyond yourself, beyond your own desires, ambitions, thoughts—the circumference of your own life—you are writing a prescription for a miserable and unhappy *existence*—not *life*, because that's not living, only *existing*. When self is master, everyone else becomes a slave.

"Me-first" people are ugly people. I don't necessarily mean in physical features. Some of the most beautiful people physically are ugly, and some of the most unattractive people physically are beautiful because they have a beautiful spirit shining through. The best beauty in all the earth is the spirit of the person shining through—a spirit of love, unselfishness, willingness, availability, dependability and Christlikeness.

"Me-first" people are unattractive.

I repeat, "me-first" people are unattractive. They are full of blemishes, and usually they are very destructive in their thoughts and actions. They are jealous, self-centered, self-serving and self-oriented.

Judas was a "me-first" person, and at the root of his dastardly deed was selfishness—greed. He clutched the bag, held onto the money, and sold Jesus Christ for the price of a slave.

Ananias and Sapphira were "me-first" people, and at the

root of their real estate deal was selfishness. You know the story. In Acts 4, the people were selling all their possessions and bringing the money and placing it at the apostles' feet. In Acts 5, Ananias came in, plunked down *x*-number of dollars. Peter said, "Wait a minute! Didn't you sell your house for such and such?"

"Yes."

"You kept back part of the price of the land. You have lied to the Holy Spirit."

Ananias took a deep breath, and that was it. It was all over. God deals very severely with people who lie to Him.

Then his wife came strutting in and told the same lie. Peter said, "Wait a minute. The feet of them which have buried your husband are waiting at the door to transport your body out." And she died instantly. An accomplice to a lie to the Holy Spirit is in a dangerous position.

My daddy once engaged Cecil Simmons, an evangelist, for a revival meeting. He had a famous sermon on tithing. On this particular Sunday morning Dr. Simmons gave an invitation something like this: "Now I want all of you who tithe to come forward and stand." (He had preached on Acts, chapter 5, about Ananias and how God killed him.)

People lined up at the front. One fellow came. I did not believe he was altogether truthful in what he was saying about his tithing. Cecil Simmons said to the people, "Now, do you know what God does to people who lie? He kills them."

About this time, the old boy started shaking. He got really white. His knees started knocking. Then out he went like a light. Four men carried him out. He didn't die, but that incident certainly put the fear of God into a lot of people.

"Me-first" people who lie to God and who are selfish have at the root of all their dealings greed and covetousness.

The rich fool was a "me-first" person, and at the root of

his foolish reasoning was selfishness. 'Soul, you have much goods laid up for many years. Take thine ease. Eat, drink and be merry. You've got a long time to live.' But like a bolt of lightning, God brought him to the end of his way that night, and Jesus posed the question: "Then whose shall those things be, which thou hast provided?"

Clutching material things brings misery and unhappiness to the Christian. So the first thing greed does is to turn a person's mind toward himself.

Second, greed tightens a person's fist and ties a knot in his purse strings. Giving is a joy. Whether you are giving love, energy, time, money or talent, giving is

| **Giving is a joy.** |

a joyful experience, while selfishness robs people of the joy of giving.

Jesus said, "It is more blessed to give than to receive." And if you follow my text, Luke 6:38, "Give, and it shall be given unto you," you can understand what Jesus meant. When you give, it will be given to you—giving you a double blessing—a blessing for giving and then getting in on the receiving end of it.

God brings joy, peace, happiness and blessing when we learn the principle of giving. When the spirit of the *Saviour* comes in, the spirit of *selfishness* goes out, and the greedy *getter* becomes a gracious *giver*. There is no principle like the principle of giving and seeing a multiple return.

You and I are sons of God by faith in Christ. So when the Saviour comes in, the spirit of greediness, that ugly "me-first" spirit, should go out.

A lot of people are suffering from a dreaded disease known as "get-itis." Did you ever hear that name? It's bad. It's destructive. It will finally kill a person. "Get-itis" means one has too much "get" in his life and not enough "give"— always getting and never giving.

The pressure of getting ties a man in knots. It ties his

spirit, his nerves and his central nervous system, while the pleasure of giving releases him for freedom and efficiency. The person with "get-itis" has a basic philosophy in life: Get all you can, can all you get and sit on the lid.

Only the Great Physician can operate on your heart and life and cure you from that awful, dreaded disease. When you get a dose of old-fashioned religion, you will get over your "get-itis." If you just have "churchanity" or if you are in the program to play along and be a part of it, forget it. But if you have Christ in your heart, the spirit of giving is in your life, and it manifests itself in giving love, joy, time, energy and strength. Everything you have just sort of oozes out because you are like Jesus.

The fussy, grumpy, grouchy, touchy, sour-faced, tight-fisted, dried-up souls are those who always put the accent on getting. God did not intend for your life to be a *reservoir* but a *channel*. God never wants us to store up but to pass on. God wants our lives to be channels through which He can bless others.

The text says, "Give, and it shall be given unto you; good measure, pressed down, and shaken together, and running over, shall men [dump into your lap]." The Bible says, "...give into your bosom," but I don't think I'm doing any injustice to the Scripture to say that God will have men just dump the returns into your lap when you learn to give.

Selfishness is a most unhappy condition, and the pastor who does not teach and train his people to give is doing them a grave injustice. They miss out on so many blessings. "It is more blessed to give than to receive." When you shut up your *outflow*, your *intake* becomes your *downfall*, and you drown yourself in the cesspool of self-centeredness.

Third, greed twists a person's per-spective out of balance. When your

> "It is more blessed to give than to receive."

Greed twists a person's perspective out of balance.

perspective of things is twisted, your priorities become tilted or off-balance. The problem with many Christians today is that they just don't have their priorities straight. They are not rightly lined up with their priorities. They put second things where first things ought to be.

What did Jesus say? "If any man will come after me, let him deny himself, and take up his cross, and follow me" (Matt. 16:24). When your priorities are tilted, you think only of you and yours.

There lived a man on a certain street who had a wife and two children, and this was his prayer: "Lord, bless me, my wife, our two children—us four and no more."

Down the street lived a man and his wife who had no children, and their prayer was: "Lord, bless us two; that will do."

Across the street lived a bachelor, and his prayer was: "Lord, bless me. I'm the only one, you see."

Greed turns our minds toward ourselves, tightens our fists, tilts our priorities and our perspective on life.

You remember that little poem:

> I had a little tea party
>   This afternoon at three.
> 'Twas very small—three guests in all:
>   I, myself and me.
> Myself ate all the sandwiches,
>   While I drank all the tea.
> 'Twas also I who ate the pie
>   And passed the cake to me.

Many people are living in that small of a perimeter—nobody but me. Just me. Greed puts a sting in your tongue. It puts envy in your soul and misery in your heart. God help us never to be "me-first," greedy, selfish, self-oriented, self-centered people. It is so much unlike Christ, for if

Christianity is anything, it is a spirit of unselfishness.

II. HOW TO OVERCOME GREED

I believe there are three steps you must take to overcome greed:

Step 1. Determine the source of your greed. Now watch this carefully. All greed, all covetousness and all selfishness stem from man's number one problem: S-I-N. And because greed is a sin, we must do the same thing with greed that we do with all other sins—take it to the One who can handle it.

The Bible says, "If we confess our sins, he is faithful and just to forgive us our sins, and to cleanse us from all unrighteousness."

Step 2. Develop a set of values based on biblical principles. Many people in the world know the price of everything but the value of nothing. What about your values? What do you really value most? A hundred years from now, a lot of things we thought were absolutely, positively, undeniably important are not going to be important at all. If we are building only for time, everything we have will fade in time; but if we are building for eternity, our investment will pay eternal dividends.

A man concerned primarily with material things came to Jesus on one occasion and said, "Master, speak to my brother, that he divide the inheritance with me" (Luke 12:13).

Here is how Jesus answered: "Take heed, and beware of covetousness: for a man's life consisteth not in the abundance of the things which he possesseth" (vs. 15). On another occasion, Jesus put it this way: "Is not the life more than meat, and the body than raiment?" (Matt. 6:25).

The things of earth grow strangely dim in the light of eternity. You start on some kind of venture—an investment, a decision you must make, something you are going to do. Maybe you were wronged in some matter, so tomorrow you are going to that person to chew him out.

But do this first. On your way to see him, stop by the cross and see the anguish and suffering of the Lord Jesus and how He suffered unjustly for your sins and mine. He made the greatest investment. He invested all of eternity, all of Heaven, all of Himself and all of God. All that Heaven could ever give, Jesus Christ invested in your life and mine.

> **Making a life is far more important than making a living.**

Develop a set of values based on biblical principles, and you will discover what is really important in life. Making a *life* is far more important than making a *living*.

Step 3. Dedicate yourself to a cause that will outlast you. Give yourself; invest your life in something that will last longer than you will.

> **Dedicate yourself to a cause that will outlast you.**

"Love not the world, neither the things that are in the world. If any man love the world, the love of the Father is not in him.

"For all that is in the world, the lust of the flesh, and the lust of the eyes, and the pride of life, is not of the Father, but is of the world."—I John 2:15, 16.

Here is the clincher: "And the world passeth away, and the lust thereof: but he that doeth the will of God abideth for ever" (vs. 17). This world system is temporal. It's headed for destruction and deterioration.

Do you want to abide forever? Do God's will. The most valuable knowledge you can have is knowing God's will. The most important thing you can do is to do God's will. Invest your life in doing God's will.

Young people, there are a lot of things you can invest your life in—Hollywood, the banking world, the financial world, the industrial world, the agricultural world—but all these are going to pass away. Invest your life in something that will outlast it.

You adults, get you a cause to live for. Invest your life in a Sunday school class, in a bus route, in winning souls, in witnessing for Christ; for these things will outlast all the things of earth. Nothing else really matters but that which is eternal.

An old man had a favorite song, and it went something like this: "No house, no land do I possess, but peace and joy and thankfulness." At every service of his church, he had permission to sing that song. He would stand up and sing, "No house, no land do I possess, but peace and joy and thankfulness."

When the people got rather weary with the dear old brother's singing that in every service, they pooled their resources and bought him a house.

The next service, when the old brother stood up to sing his favorite song, he started out, "No house, no land...," and broke down. He couldn't go any further, so he sat down. The next service came, and the same thing happened. The third week when he got up to sing, "No house...," he broke down and wept uncontrollably. He no longer had a song.

Finally, upon gaining his composure, he said, "Take back the house and give me back my song."

Let me ask you: What good is a house if you don't have a song? What good are material things if you don't have the joy and peace of God?

Invest your life in something that will outlast it. Then when all of eternity has rolled its clock for the last time, you can say, "Lord, I have invested my life in the cause of Christ, and here are the jewels I am bringing Home with me."

I want to tell you one thing: When you get to Heaven,

God will not be nearly as interested in where you came from as He will in how many you brought with you.

CONCLUSION: No man lives to himself, and no man dies to himself; and every man must give an account of himself to God.

7.
ATTITUDE OF REBELLION

"For as he thinketh in his heart, so is he."—Prov. 23:7.

The text for my message is Psalm 78:1–8:

"Give ear, O my people, to my law: incline your ears to the words of my mouth.

"I will open my mouth in a parable: I will utter dark sayings of old:

"Which we have heard and known, and our fathers have told us.

"We will not hide them from their children, shewing to the generation to come the praises of the Lord, for his strength, and his wonderful works that he hath done.

"For he established a testimony in Jacob, and appointed a law in Israel, which he commanded our fathers, that they should make them known to their children:

"That the generation to come might know them, even the children which should be born; who should arise and declare them to their children:

"That they might set their hope in God, and not forget the works of God, but keep his commandments:

"And might not be as their fathers, a stubborn and rebellious generation; a generation that set not their heart aright, and whose spirit was not stedfast with God."

There is a great deal of rebellion in our day. We came through the decade of the sixties, which was probably the most rebellious decade in the history of the United States of America. If this age in which we live would bear any descriptive title, it might be that of the "Age of Rebellion." In government, in homes, in businesses, on the streets and avenues, in the highways and lanes of America, there has been, and there is, an attitude of rebellion.

Don't look now, but your attitude is showing.

I. WHAT IS REBELLION?

Webster defines *rebellion* as "a defiance of or opposition to any control." When we go in opposition to God's control over us, we place ourselves in defiance of Almighty God. Anytime you personally set yourself in opposition to authority, the control that is exercised above you—be it on the job, in the home or in the church—you are in defiance of or rebellion against authority.

According to I Samuel 15:23, "Rebellion is as the sin of witchcraft." Do you know the seriousness, the severity of the sin of witchcraft? Do you know the penalty for witchcraft? According to Exodus 22:18, one who practiced witchcraft was put to death. And according to Galatians 5:20,21, those who practice witchcraft cannot inherit the kingdom of God. And according to Revelation 22:14,15, no sorcerer (one who deals in witchcraft) shall enter the city of God.

Rebellion is defiance against the laws of God.

Being rebellious against God or against authority is a very serious business. The bottom line is this: Rebellion is defiance against the laws of God. It is tantamount to disobeying God's law, and I John 3:4 makes it plain that he who transgresses the law of God commits sin, "for sin is the transgression of the law."

Observe with me several crucial areas we might find ourselves caught up in as we breathe rebellion against God.

To disobey God's law against idolatry is rebellion.

First, to disobey God's law against idolatry (the worship of a pagan or idol god) is rebellion. That doesn't mean you have to go to India and bow down

64

before a cow or go to China and bow down before a graven image. We have our own idols, our own pagan, false, lifeless gods in America—the god of pleasure, the god of lust, the god of greed, the god of gold, the god of money, the god of "let me do what I want to do without restraint in my life." To disobey the law of God against *idolatry* is rebellion, for God says, "Thou shalt have no other gods before me."

Second, to disobey God's law of divine respect is rebellion against God, for God says, "Thou shalt not take the name of the LORD thy God in vain." To disobey the law of God governing the *respect for authority* in the world is rebellion against God.

> To disobey God's law of divine respect is rebellion.

The number one authority in the universe is the *law of God.* There is no higher appeal beyond the law of God, the written Word.

The number two authority in the world in the family structure is *parental authority.* It is a serious matter to disobey one's parents. It is a sin against God to defy the laws of one's parents, for the Bible says, "Honour thy father and thy mother: that thy days may be long upon the land."

There is a third authority. We might call it an *ecclesiastical authority* or the *church authority.* I believe the leadership, the pastor of the church, has authority in the church. That does not mean or suggest the pastor is a dictator. Some people do call their pastors dictators—"oh, he's just a dictator." I have been called a lot of things, so I don't mind that, but I have never tried to be a dictator. But there is a pastoral authority given by God, and to disobey pastoral authority is a sin against God.

God help us not to be in defiance of God's authority or the church's authority or the authority of the home.

To disobey God's law of the sanctity of life is rebellion against God. One of the commandments reads, "Thou shalt

To disobey
God's law of
the sanctity of
life is rebellion
against
God.

not kill." The word for "kill" there really makes the commandment mean "Thou shalt not murder." Think of the issue of abortion in our country. To disregard the sanctity of life, to disobey God's law, to defy God's law is rebellion against God.

To disobey God's law of morality is rebellion. The Bible says, "Thou shalt not commit adultery."

To disobey God's law of honesty is rebellion against God. The Bible says, "Thou shalt not steal."

To disobey God's law of truth is rebellion against God. The Bible says, "Thou shalt not bear false witness."

When we bring in the whole program of God's eternal, infallible and inescapable law, there are laws in the universe we cannot defy.

You can't get up on top of the Southland Life building or the Continental National Life building and step off into space without going to the ground. I don't care what kind of contact you have with the other world, you cannot defy the law of gravity.

You can't defy the laws of energy and heat. If you put your hand in fire, you are going to be burned. These irrevocable, inescapable laws of God cannot be violated without paying the consequences.

There are those in our world who say they do not believe God exists. They say that God, if He ever lived, is dead.

"God is dead," the theologians say;
But I know He's not: I talked with Him today.
"Dead, never to live again," they claim—
But alive to save through His Son's dear name.
"Alive! Alive!" let it be said:
God will be living when the theologians are dead.

God is alive, and no thought of God's decease or demise

or nonexistence will ever change that unalterable fact.

I read an amusing story about a man who had called a great crowd together. He was going on in his great tirade against religion and God and the Bible, saying, "I'm going to call God to a showdown. I'm going to challenge God." So he gathered this great crowd of people around him, stood on the mountainside, shook his fist toward Heaven, and said, "God, if there is such a person, if there is a God, send the lightning and strike me dead."

Since God had already made a commitment to a bunch of little boys and girls that He would give them fair weather for a picnic, He sent along a little gnat. It got lodged in the man's throat and choked him to death.

God is still alive! He is controlling the universe. His laws are unalterable and inescapable. And we must come to the point where we will obey the law of God.

II. WHEN DID REBELLION BEGIN?

When did rebellion begin in the universe? Isaiah, chapter 14, is one of the most amazing chapters in the Bible. I will read verses 12 through 15:

"How art thou fallen from heaven, O Lucifer, son of the morning! How art thou cut down to the ground, which didst weaken the nations!

"For thou hast said in thine heart, I will ascend into heaven, I will exalt my throne above the stars of God: I will sit also upon the mount of the congregation, in the sides of the north:

"I will ascend above the heights of the clouds; I will be like the most High.

"Yet thou shalt be brought down to hell, to the sides of the pit."

> **We cannot defy God without paying the price.**

We cannot defy God, we cannot rebel against God, without paying the price.

Jesus said in the Gospel according to Luke, "I beheld

Satan as lightning fall from heaven" (Luke 10:18). The first rebellion against God, then, was by the Devil himself, Lucifer, the son of the morning, who said, "I will exalt my throne above the stars of God."

The first manifestation of rebellion in the human race took place in the Garden of Eden.

Turn to Genesis, chapter 3, the book of origins, the book of beginnings. This is the sad saga of Satan's dirtiest deed:

"Now the serpent was more subtil than any beast of the field which the LORD God had made. And he said unto the woman, Yea, hath God said, Ye shall not eat of every tree of the garden?

"And the woman said unto the serpent, We may eat of the fruit of the trees of the garden:

"But of the fruit of the tree which is in the midst of the garden, God hath said, Ye shall not eat of it, neither shall ye touch it, lest ye die.

"And the serpent said unto the woman, Ye shall not surely die:

"For God doth know that in the day ye eat thereof, then your eyes shall be opened, and ye shall be as gods, knowing good and evil.

"And when the woman saw that the tree was good for food, and that it was pleasant to the eyes, and a tree to be desired to make one wise, she took of the fruit thereof, and did eat, and gave also unto her husband with her; and he did eat.

"And the eyes of them both were opened, and they knew that they were naked; and they sewed fig leaves together, and made themselves aprons.

"And they heard the voice of the Lord God walking in the garden in the cool of the day: and Adam and his wife hid themselves from the presence of the Lord God amongst the trees of the garden.

"And the Lord God called unto Adam, and said unto him, Where art thou?

"And he said, I heard thy voice in the garden, and I was afraid, because I was naked; and I hid myself.

"And he said, Who told thee that thou wast naked? Hast thou eaten of the tree, whereof I commanded thee that thou shouldest not eat?

"And the man said, The woman whom thou gavest to be with me, she gave me of the tree, and I did eat.

"And the LORD God said unto the woman, What is this that thou hast done? And the woman said, The serpent beguiled me, and I did eat."—Vss. 1–13.

They were passing the buck from one to the other. We are always blaming someone else. If things don't go right on the job, we come home and blame the wife and children, kick the dog and throw out the cat. Look in the mirror, my friend, and see where the problem is. Don't blame the world. Don't blame the wife. Don't blame the family. Blame yourself.

From then until now there has been rebellion in the human race. There has been rebellion on the part of groups and on the part of individuals. Let me give you one classic example of each.

In Numbers 16, Korah, Dathan and Abiram brought 250 people together to Moses and Aaron and said, "Moses and Aaron, you are taking too much authority around here. We think we ought to have some of that authority. You have elevated yourselves, and you have taken it in your hands to tell all this great congregation what to do and when they can do it; and you don't deserve that authority."

Moses said, "Oh, is that right? Well, I'll tell you what we will do. We'll let God decide. You get your men and get your fire holders and bring incense and fire and stand before the congregation of the Lord. If God honors you, then we will turn the authority over to you."

And so they did. God smiled upon Moses and Aaron and disapproved of the rebellion of Korah, Dathan and Abiram.

Moses said, "Now, Lord, just to make sure nobody will misunderstand this matter, if these men are wrong in rebelling against divinely appointed authority, open up the earth and swallow up Korah and all that appertain to him."

God said, "All right, Moses. Get your men on the other side of the creek, because something is about to happen."

And all of a sudden, the earth opened and swallowed Korah and all who appertained unto him, and fire lapped out and consumed the 250 men who had offered incense—all because they rebelled against God!

> It is a dangerous thing to rebel against the authority of God.

It is a dangerous thing to rebel against the authority of God.

One incident of an individual's rebelling against parental authority is that of the Prodigal Son in Luke 15. It is as though he said, "I don't need Mother and Dad's restraint any longer. I'm a big boy now. I can go my own way, do my own thing. Give me that which belongs to me."

It is a dangerous hour when a young man or woman rises up in rebellion against the authority of a mother and father. It is something that will live with you all the days of your life. God help you. The Prodigal Son was brought to the hogpen.

III. HOW TO OVERCOME REBELLION

How can one overcome the spirit of rebellion, defiance? I'm not talking about going out with a hammer and a gun in hand and rebelling and defying authority. No, I am talking about the attitude of your heart!

Remember, the basis of this whole series of messages is Proverbs 23:7, "For as he thinketh in his heart, so is he."

> There is always a penalty for wrong.

The wrong attitude ends up with the wrong deportment, the wrong conduct, the wrong behavior; and there is always a penalty for wrong.

Are you battling with rebellion? Young people, do you sometimes feel a little rebellion in your heart against Mother's authority or Dad's authority? Do you feel a little rebellion against the authority of government or the authority of the church? Is there just a bit of a rebellious spirit toward authority?

Let me suggest three things to overcome it: Admit that rebellion in any form is a sin against God and repent of it. Yield yourself as an obedient servant of God to obey Him in everything in life. Surrender your will to God's will.

Now, when you put these three together—admitting rebellion is a sin; yielding your life, your way, your spirit to God's Spirit; and surrendering your will to God's will—you can overcome even the tinges of rebellion that might be creeping into the northeast corner of your mind. Just thinking about some way you might want to rebel against authority is a dangerous thing. Don't let it happen. Have a kind, contrite, humble spirit.

In I Samuel 15 is a classic example. God sent Saul on a mission, and the mission was to wipe out the Amalekites, both man and beast. When Saul saw some of the fat cattle and the beautiful sheep, he decided he would keep the best of them for himself.

Along came Samuel, the prophet of God. Samuel said to Saul, "Have you done what God told you to do?"

"Oh, yes."

"You have killed all the Amalekites?"

"Oh, yes."

"You have destroyed all the beasts, all the cattle, all the sheep?"

"Oh, yes." About that time a little sheep went, "Baa, baa."

Samuel asked Saul, "What meaneth then the bleating of the sheep? You have defied God's law, disobeyed Him and rebelled against the commandment of God."

When King Saul was reproved by the Prophet Samuel, he confessed, saying, "I have sinned."

There will never be victory until we are willing to say, "Lord, I have sinned." Take inventory of your life. Right now recall in your own mind the one sin that troubles you. Then say to the Lord, "I have sinned." Plead the blood of Jesus Christ. Ask for forgiveness; and God's mercy, kindness and patience will be extended toward you.

CONCLUSION: He who rebels against the Light will be lost in eternal darkness.

Don't let the sin, the attitude of rebellion, destroy your life. It will if you don't get it under control.

8.
ATTITUDE OF WORRY

"For as he thinketh in his heart, so is he."—Prov. 23:7.

My text for this hour is Philippians 4:6–9. There Paul writes:

"Be careful for nothing; but in every thing by prayer and supplication with thanksgiving let your requests be made known unto God.

"And the peace of God, which passeth all understanding, shall keep your hearts and minds through Christ Jesus.

"Finally, brethren, whatsoever things are true, whatsoever things are honest, whatsoever things are just, whatsoever things are pure, whatsoever things are lovely, whatsoever things are of good report; if there be any virtue, and if there be any praise, think on these things.

"Those things, which ye have both learned, and received, and heard, and seen in me, do: and the God of peace shall be with you."

Three exciting words jump off the page to the discerning reader of these verses: **prayer, think, do**—pray right, think right, do right. In this message, I hope all of us will be able to discern what is causing us to worry, what worry is, how it affects us and how we can overcome it.

> **Pray right,
> think right,
> do right.**

The book of Philippians is known as the psychology book of the Bible. In his writing to the church at Philippi, Paul dwells much on their thoughts, their minds. He said, "The peace of God which passeth all understanding, shall keep your hearts and minds." And we have that famous verse, "Let this mind be in you, which was also in Christ Jesus" (Phil. 2:5).

I need not tell you that billions of dollars, thousands of books, hundreds of seminars and dozens of courses are offered in the various areas of life on how to conquer worry. I wish we had all the money in our coffers that has been spent on books that have been written from a secular point of view on how to overcome worry. Yet the Apostle Paul gives it to us in one single verse: "Be careful [anxious] for nothing; but in every thing by prayer and supplication with thanksgiving let your requests be made known unto God."

In other words, Paul is saying, "Here it is, folks. You don't have to attend all the seminars, read all the books, go to all the places where somebody has set up a podium to tell you how to think your way positively to success." Now that is all right as far as it goes, but the human element is not enough. We must have the mind of Christ in order to conquer fear, frustration, worry and all these other things that come into our lives.

What do you have to worry about? If you do not have a million dollars, you never have to worry about losing a million dollars.

What are you worrying about? Are you worrying about the economy? The child of God is on a different economy from this world. If you haven't learned that, you have never learned to live. If you haven't learned that God, in some way, in some manner, somehow unknown to man, can take care of your needs, you haven't yet learned to live. It's thrilling when you know God has you on another economy. He said in Philippians 4:19, "But my God shall supply all your need."

If God promises to supply all my needs, that's all I need. I am going to trust Him for it. All I need is all I need.

Are you worrying about depression? Some of you remember those Depression days from 1929 into the 1930s. I'm a Depression kid myself. I know what it was like to have nine children in the family and Dad on a very limited income. I can remember times when he came home with five dollars to feed eleven people. I know what it is; but I remember that the psalmist said, "I have been young, and now am old; yet have I not seen the righteous forsaken, nor his seed begging bread" (37:25).

Depression may come, but God can feed us, clothe us and give us a place to live. After all, those are the basics anyhow. God never promised to supply all you want but all you need. Some of you have your "wanter" going all the time, but He said He would supply all your **needs**.

Are you worrying about the **past?** Nothing you can do will change the past. All the problems, all the scars, all the heartache, all the things that have happened can't be changed; so don't spend time worrying about what was. Today is the day. Now is the time.

Are you worrying about the **future?** Jesus said, and Paul quotes Him in Hebrews 13:5,6:

"Let your conversation be without covetousness; and be content with such things as ye have: for he hath said, I will never leave thee, nor forsake thee.

"So that we may boldly say, The Lord is my helper, and I will not fear what man shall do unto me."

Don't worry about the future.

We worry about whether we are going to have cancer; whether the economy is going to stay up; whether gold or silver is going to stay up. We worry about our jobs. We worry about our houses. Worry is very close to discouragement. Usually people who worry all the time stay discouraged.

Here are ten of the greatest rules to cure the blues: **Go out and do something for somebody else and repeat that nine times.** Do that, and you will overcome all your discouragement and all your blues.

If anybody had reason to worry, it was the Apostle

Paul. His Christian friends were fighting in the church at Philippi almost to the point of splitting it. How sad when churches split.

I read about a Virginia church that split because of a difference in the time! The pastor asked, "What time is it?" One woman said, "It's 7:28." Another woman said, "It's 7:29." And they had a fight and a split in the church over one minute!

Paul's friends were fussing, and they almost split the church. He was in prison and facing death by execution. He hadn't seen his friends for a long time. Paul was growing old. He had no Social Security, no Medicaid, no Medicare, no retirement program, no burial insurance, no hospitalization, no bank account, no savings bonds, no vacation pay. In fact, he never had a vacation, to say nothing of the pay.

Paul didn't have a cemetery lot. I wonder where they buried him. They cut his head off, but that was just a shortcut to Glory. Just like that, Paul was in Glory! He had already written, 'To be absent from the body is to be present with the Lord.'

Now to add to all these things Paul could worry about, he was chained to a Roman soldier.

With all these worries or things that were potential worries and problems to Paul, he could yet write in Philippians 4:4, "Rejoice in the Lord alway: and again I say, Rejoice." Nineteen times in the book of Philippians Paul uses the word "joy" or "rejoice," and he uses "weeping" only twice. It's a book of rejoicing.

I. WHAT IS WORRY?

The word *worry* comes from an ancient English word, an Anglo-Saxon word meaning "to choke or to strangle." When somebody has you around the neck, cutting off the wind—that is precisely what the word *worry* means. It strangles, it chokes your emotional life. Worry is a destroyer, a crippler, a killer. Hard work has never killed anybody, but worry has. Someone said, "Worry is interest paid on trouble before it is due."

There are those who worry about three kinds of trouble: (1) all the trouble they ever had; (2) all the trouble they have now; (3) all the trouble they ever expect to have.

> Worry is a destroyer, a crippler, a killer.

Some people, when they go to bed at night, take a certain medicine just in case otherwise a headache would develop during the night or they would get up with a headache. That's advance preparation.

Dear me! God has never made a Christian strong enough to carry all of today's duties with tomorrow's worries piled on top of them. The poet said:

Do not trouble trouble, 'til trouble troubles you,
For you only make your troubles double trouble when
   you do.

Do not look for trouble; let trouble look for you.

Don't go around with a spyglass looking for something to worry about.

I used to teach a psychology class. A young man in the class would come and tell all the things he had worried about. We had in class gone through all these steps, and we thought, *Man! He is on top of the situation!*

One day he came in with this worried look on his face. I asked, "Son, why are you worrying again today?" He said, "Well, I am worried because I can't think of anything to worry about."

O dear me! God help us! "Let this mind be in you, which was also in Christ Jesus."

There are three days in every week when you should never worry: yesterday, today and tomorrow.

One guy I knew fixed up a little box with a hole on top, and he called it his Wednesday Worry Box. On Thursday he wrote down his worry for that day, put it in that box and said he wouldn't worry about that until next Wednesday. Friday, Saturday, Sunday—every day—the same, his worry for each day was put in the Wednesday Worry Box. When Wednesday came, he would open the box. Lo and behold, most of the things he thought he had to worry about had never happened. They just vanished, and he didn't have anything to worry about!

Let's fix up a Wednesday Worry Box. Put your worries in a box and worry about them next Wednesday.

A survey shows that ninety-two percent of all things people worry about never actually happen. Worry is like a rocking chair; it gives you something to do but gets you nowhere.

Now some people really prefer to worry. They would rather worry than do most anything else. In fact, they just get really worried if there is nothing to worry them. They really thrive on this business of worry.

Now suppose you are a teenager. You are five-feet-two-inches tall. Your lifelong ambition is to be a professional basketball player. There are two things you can do about it: **smile** or **cry**. Smiling will not make you six-feet-eight-inches tall, nor will crying. Jesus said in Matthew 6:27 that you can't add anything to your stature. You can worry, become bitter, develop a complex; but you cannot grow eighteen inches by worrying about it.

Imagine some things that might happen to you tomorrow. You might break a foot or get fired. Your hair dryer might short out and burn off all your hair. Your pet rabbit may die. Your pet mouse may develop cancer from eating too many cyclamates. But worrying is certainly not going to help.

Consider the birds. We can learn a lot from birds. They have no stores, no banks, no factories, no cars, no insurance policies; yet the birds don't sit around and sulk, fret and worry. Did you ever know a bird to fly up to the tallest limb of a tall Texas pine and jump off and kill himself? Anybody ever know a bird to do that? Birds don't worry.

> Said the Robin to the Sparrow:
>   "I should really like to know
> Why these anxious human beings
>   Rush about and worry so."
> Said the Sparrow to the Robin:
>   "Friend, I think that it must be
> That they have no Heavenly Father
>   Such as cares for you and me."

Not even a sparrow, worth so little, can fall without God's knowledge.

People worry their way through life because they think they are unimportant and useless. They look in the mirror every day and go down the list citing all their miseries: "I'm just a dummy. People don't even like me. I'm going to flunk geology. I've got a terminal case of dandruff."

My friend, even if all these things are so, you are still important. You are made in the likeness and image of God. Jesus Christ died for you. You are the prize possession of the Father, the apple of His eye and useful in this society.

Now had Jesus said, "I will never leave you until day after tomorrow," you would have something to worry about. But He said, "I will never leave thee, nor forsake thee."

Worry is a sickness. The divine Physician has a remedy in these two things in the prescription:

> **Worry is a sickness.**

(1) "Seek ye first the kingdom of God, and his righteousness." I challenge you to put God, the church and the cause of Christ first in your life. Then tell me He doesn't meet your needs.

Somebody says, "I'm just afraid I can't meet my bills if I tithe." I tell you, you can't meet your bills if you don't tithe. Somebody says, "I just don't have enough to go around." You've got to start in the right place: honor God with the firstfruits of your income, your time, your energy, your talent and all you have. Seek first His kingdom.

(2) **Learn to live one day at a time.** I have several clocks in my house. I love clocks and bells. The grandfather clock

Learn to live one day at a time.

ticks and ticks and ticks and keeps on ticking. It may tick for a hundred years, but it will tick only **one** tick at a time. You must learn to live one day at a time.

Jesus taught His disciples to pray. I imagine the disciples said, "Lord, we want to have everything mapped out for at least twelve months."

Jesus said, 'When you get down to pray, you pray, Our Father which is in Heaven, hallowed be Thy name; Thy kingdom come, Thy will be done, on earth as it is in Heaven. Give us enough to last for twelve months.' Is that what He said? No. The prayer was, "Give us *this day* our daily bread." The disciples were living in times of persecution. They might not even be alive in twelve months. If God dishes it out day by day, that's all we need. You can't use any more than you can use today. Learn to live one day at a time.

Worry is a pagan practice. Worry won't make you a

Worry is a pagan practice.

pagan, but worry will produce a Christian who has a pagan practice. The bottom line: Worry is a sin.

Do I have proof of that? I surely do. From Romans 14:23 I will prove that worry is a sin—a sin whatever form it comes in. You can wrap it up any way you want to, but sin is sin; and worry is a sin.

> **Worry is a sin.**

Listen: "And he that doubteth is damned if he eat, because he eateth not of faith: for whatsoever is not of faith is sin." Worry is not of faith. I'm concluding logically from what the Word of God says: Since worry is not of faith, then worry is a sin.

> **Worry is not of faith.**

II. HOW DOES WORRY AFFECT US?

It attacks the whole personality. It reduces the level of achievement, depletes the body, robs you of sleep, takes away your appetite, cuts down on your efficiency. It causes heart trouble. It gives you neck pain, back pain, leg pain, head pain, indigestion and ulcers. Worry will affect you mentally, spiritually, physically and emotionally.

Worry, hurry, bury—the first two lead to the third. Worry wastes your body, cankers your soul, rusts your heart, dampens your spirit, dulls your mind and spoils your disposition. Worry will make you irritable, gloomy, impatient and ill-tempered. Worry clouds your personal happiness and damages your social relationships.

I read something I thought was very interesting. During World War I, the army fliers developed this philosophy: When you are in the air, you will either be flying straight or turning over. If you are flying straight, there is no cause to worry. If you are turning over, one of two things is true: you will either right the plane or fall. If you right the plane, there is no cause to worry. If you fall, one of two things is certain: you will either be injured slightly or injured seriously. If you are injured slightly, there is no need to worry. If you are injured seriously, one of two things will happen: you will either die or recover. If you recover, there is no need to worry. If you die, you can't worry.

If we faced life like that—had that kind of philosophy—there would be nothing to worry about.

There are four main causes for worry: (1) **thinking** of what you do not have instead of thinking of what you do have; (2) **refusing** to face life as it is; (3) **centering** your thoughts on yourself instead of on those about you; (4) **failing** to exercise faith in God.

III. HOW TO OVERCOME WORRY

Here is the real core of the message: **How can a person overcome worry?** Not by drugs, not by alcohol, not by mental gymnastics, not by sedatives and tranquilizers, not by making new resolutions. Isaiah said, "Thou wilt keep him in perfect peace, whose mind is stayed on thee: because he trusteth in thee" (26:3).

God has a divine prescription, and it is found in my text. Three things are involved in Philippians 4:

> The right kind of praying, right kind of thinking, right kind of living

(1) The right kind of praying;

(2) The right kind of thinking;

(3) The right kind of living.

Why is prayer such an important, effective and vital therapy in overcoming worry? The chief cause of worry is always thinking about self. Prayer directs your thoughts away from self and toward God. You cannot think about God and self at the same time. So prayer puts your thoughts where they belong.

"Set your affection on things above" (Col. 3:2). "Let this mind be in you, which was also in Christ Jesus" (Phil. 2:5). The only way you can do that is with **the right kind of praying.**

Second, **the right kind of thinking**. Paul said, "If there be any virtue,…think on these things." What things? "Whatsoever things are true, whatsoever things are honest, whatsoever things are just, whatsoever things are pure, whatsoever things are lovely, whatsoever things are of good report; …think on these things."

If you think bad things all the time, you will go to bed worrying about all the bad things that happened. Then you will wake up with a bitter taste in your mouth. Don't think on negative things. Rather, think on these things: what is pure, lovely, honorable, just, honest, of good report.

Then in verse 9 we have **the right kind of living**: "Those things, which ye have both learned, and received, and heard, and seen in me, do." In verses 6–9 you have underlined *prayer, think, do*. Just to **pray right** is not enough. Just to **think right** is not enough. You have to **do right**. And you will never do right unless you are thinking right and praying right.

> **You have to do right.**

Why did Paul put them in that order? Was that an accident? No. First, the right kind of **praying**; second, the right kind of **thinking**; and third, the right kind of **doing** or the right kind of **living**. James said, "Be ye doers of the word, and not hearers only."

CONCLUSION: Pray right, think right, do right, and then you will **be** right. Now, you don't have anything else to worry about, because I'm through! Worry is a sin, and if the peace of God is **guarding your life** and the Spirit of God is **guiding your life**, then the Son of God will be **keeping your life**.

9.
ATTITUDE OF FEAR

"For as he thinketh in his heart, so is he."—Prov. 23:7.

Our text for this message is II Timothy 1:7:

"For God hath not given us the spirit of fear; but of power, and of love, and of a sound mind."

Inasmuch as God has given us freedom from fear, logically we can follow through with saying we can possess a sound mind.

Paul wrote to the church at Philippi, "Let this mind be in you, which was also in Christ Jesus."

Don't look now, but your attitude is showing.

One of the first emotions experienced by man was the emotion of fear. Genesis 3:10 records the first words Adam spoke after the Fall in the Garden of Eden: "I heard thy voice in the garden, and I was afraid." From then until this hour, in all areas of the world, from every continent, every climate, every culture, every civilization, every city, every village, every street, and from all walks of life, men have been gripped by fear.

In Luke 21:26, our Lord Jesus said about the last days: "Men's hearts failing them for fear, and for looking after those things which are coming on the earth."

Look around you. Do you see anyone, anywhere, completely free of fear? The wealthy man with all his money, comfortably situated in his mansion, has this horrendous fear that he is going to lose his mind. The housewife's neighbor just died of cancer, and though she has gotten a clean bill of health and everything is all right, she still has that intense fear that she too will have cancer. The young athlete on the playing field has this awesome fear that a broken bone will sideline him for the rest of the season and perhaps end his sports career.

Look closely at all those faces in the crowd lining the streets of our city, the crowds in the supermarkets or the shopping centers or the train stations or the airports. Fear is written deeply and with capital letters all over their countenances. But why study all the faces in the crowd? Why not go home and look in the mirror, for you are also afraid?

We are living in an age of fear. When historians write about the late twentieth century they will write about a generation, a culture, a civilization characterized by fear. In the university of life, most all the students belong to one fraternity, the **fraternity of fear.** Fear is no respecter of persons. Fear strikes the rich and the poor, the learned and the unlearned, the sophisticated and the unsophisticated, the famous and the infamous. All men everywhere drink at the fountain of fear.

> **Fear is no respecter of persons.**

I have four basic questions in my message:

I. WHAT IS FEAR?

The dictionary defines *fear* as "a painful emotion marked by alarm." A second dictionary definition is: "Fear is what one feels in the presence of real or assumed danger." I like best this definition: "Fear is the darkroom where negatives are developed."

There are basically two kinds of fears: real fears and imaginary fears. Real fears are normal, legitimate, useful and helpful. On the other hand, imaginary fears are abnormal, illegitimate and pathological in nature. Real fear preserves life, while imaginary fears destroy it. Real fear is a friend; imaginary fears are foes. Let me give you an example.

To be afraid of an onrushing car, out of control, with a nut behind the wheel, is a normal fear. Something would be wrong with you if you weren't afraid of that. But to be so afraid of the car that might be out of control somewhere down the highway or down the street, that you never cross the street, is an abnormal fear, and the person who has that fear has some real problems.

When does a normal fear become an abnormal fear? A normal, logical, legitimate fear becomes an abnormal, illogical, illegitimate fear when you park by it; for then **fear becomes anxiety.**

Many imaginary fears plague us. Let me mention some of them that are more familiar to you, like claustrophobia (a fear of closed-in places) or hydrophobia (a fear of water). I've met a few people who I felt were so afraid of water they never chose to take a bath!

Agoraphobia (the fear of open spaces) is one of the fears that grip a lot of people. Literally thousands of people in the United States never go out their front doors because they have this morbid, subnormal, illogical, illegitimate fear of open spaces.

My wife's folks live in New Mexico, so just about every summer we go to New Mexico. We've driven by the sandy crest and the tramway that goes up thousands of feet. Every year I say, "One day I'm going to ride it. Someday I'm going to get on it." Well, this year we rode it. Every time a bit of wind came and blew the tramcar, my heart skipped a bit. I am just a little afraid of high places. I can get in an airplane and go as high and as fast as they go, but when I get on something swinging on a cable like this, I get a little afraid.

Then there is zoophobia (the fear of animals).

Acrophobia is the fear of high places.

Another is autophobia (the fear of being alone). Some people just can't be alone.

One you may not be familiar with is gamophobia (the fear of marriage). You didn't know there was such a fear? I know some guys who have been afraid ever since they got married!

Then there is thanatophobia, from the word *thanatopsis* (the fear of death).

Then there is necrophobia (the fear of dead bodies).

Many years ago we had a maid working in our home who was terribly afraid to go into a home where there was a dead body. Back in those days people usually took the corpses back home and had the wakes in their homes. Mother said to her, "Nanny Lee, I've prepared a dish, and I want you to take it up to the neighbor's house where there's been a death."

"Oh no," she said. "Mrs. Barber, I-I-I..."

My mother said, "Now, Nanny Lee, a dead body won't hurt you."

"I know, Mrs. Barber, but they sure can make you hurt yourself."

Fears of all kinds, abnormal fears, reduce us to timid, ineffective cowards, unable to face life.

Edward Spencer Coles said, "Fear claims more victims, causes more suffering, injures more family circles, costs the state and industry more money annually than cancer, tuberculosis and syphilis combined."

I'm dealing with a real enemy tonight—the enemy called fear. It is so costly. It has paralyzed so many people, caused so many heartaches, hindered and retarded the development and the growth of so many people emotionally, that we must come to grips with this enemy.

Mark Twain said, "I've had a lot of troubles in my life, and ninety percent of them never happened." These things we are afraid of usually never happen.

Now, very innocently, parents will say to their little children, "Don't you go into that dark room. A bogeyman will get you." And some adults are afraid to go in a dark room because they think a bogeyman is in there. Don't teach people an abnormal fear. There is absolutely nothing wrong with the dark that should cause us to be afraid, so don't instill that in your children.

Internationally there are fears. The nations of earth are asking about the nuclear bomb. Which nations have it? That causes international fear.

There are national fears—the economy, depression, inflation, all of these things.

There are personal fears—disaster, disease and death.

It is evident that the source of our fears is not God. God has not given us the spirit of fear. Then, if our fears are not from God, they stem from the feelings of guilt and inadequacy and from sin. If they are not of God, then it is evident that the Devil has put these unnatural, abnormal, illogical fears in your heart in order to rob you of your Christian joy and to neutralize you as an effective servant of Jesus Christ.

> **God has not given us the spirit of fear.**

Jesus said in Matthew 10:28, "Fear not them which kill the body, but are not able to kill the soul: but rather fear him which is able to destroy both soul and body in hell." The psalmist said, "I will not fear what flesh can do unto me" (Ps. 56:4).

II. OF WHAT ARE PEOPLE AFRAID?

A little girl said to her daddy, "Daddy, are you afraid of long, woolly worms?"

He replied, "No, darling, I'm not."

"Well, Daddy, are you afraid of a big brown cow?"

"No, darling, I'm not."

"Well, Daddy, you are not afraid of anything but Mama, are you?"

A survey shows that twenty-four out of twenty-five people are afraid of something, real or unreal. One in ten is afraid of the dark. One in four is afraid of animals, mostly mice. I'm one in the four who is afraid of mice.

When we first moved to where we now live, all the fields out there were open, and there were some field mice. During the first cool spell, the field mice wanted to find a little warm place, so one little field mouse (so small it couldn't even trip the trap) got in through the garage and into the kitchen and underneath the sink.

Finally, my wife (I'm afraid of the trap, to say nothing of the mouse) finagled with the trap until she got it to where the least little thing would trip it. She put this hunk of cheese on it and set it down.

One night, in the quiet of the den, we heard this little click, and I said, "There's your mouse!" My wife prevailed upon me to get the mouse out. I opened the cabinet, looked, and I said, "Now, Lord, You know You didn't call me to do this!" I looked and looked at that mouse. Finally an idea came. I went into the garage and got a six-foot, long-handled shovel. (You don't think I'm afraid of mice?) That mouse was a tiny field mouse caught in a trap; and I got a long-handled shovel, went in and quietly shoveled the mouse out and threw it outside! Ultimately my wife had to retrieve the trap.

One in five is afraid of heights, spaces and water. Four out of five are afraid of failure, humiliation, ridicule and their own inadequacies. The list goes on—disease, death, war, depression, fire, flood, tornadoes, lightning and losing jobs. (A recent survey shows ninety-five percent of those people who lost their jobs found better ones.) Fear of losing health, your home, your mind, your money, being alone, facing old age, talking to the boss man; fear of the end of the world, of the future...but wait! Don't fear the future. God is already there.

The two natural, inbred, innate fears we are all born with, primarily and basically, are the fear of falling and the fear of loud noises. All these other fears are picked up somewhere along the way. Some of our fears are totally logical; some are totally illogical.

A man tells of the time his wife awakened him in the middle of the night, crying hysterically. When he finally calmed her down and asked why she was crying so, her answer was, "I'm afraid our son is going to be killed in the war."

Is that illogical? Yes, when you realize their son was four years old and fast asleep in the next room! So her husband said, "It will be at least fifteen years before he can go to war, and I think this war will be over by then." Illogical fears.

There are two things we should never fear: the things we can change (if you can change it, don't be afraid of it); the things we cannot change. So bringing it down to the narrowest point—why should we fear?

Here are three guidelines for us to follow: trust God, help others and live one day at a time.

> Trust God, help others and live one day at a time.

III. HOW DOES FEAR AFFECT PEOPLE?

Medical science estimates that from sixty to ninety

percent of all sicknesses are caused either by fear, sorrow, envy, resentment or hatred. Fear is listed first. Fear paralyzes the spirit, binds the mind, enslaves the will, weakens the body and poisons the soul.

Fear and worry live in the same cell, and they work together to reduce your level of achievement, to cut back on your spirit of adventure, and to restrict your accomplishments in life.

Doctors will tell you that many hospital beds are filled with those who have no organic illness whatsoever, but they are functionally incapacitated because of fear. So it is possible to be so fear-ridden that you may become bedridden, literally paralyzed by fear, rendered ineffective and unable to function. Fear robs one of his sleep, tenses one's nerves, disturbs the digestion and causes many psychosomatic illnesses.

IV. HOW CAN WE OVERCOME FEAR?

We have seen what fear is; we have seen what some of the fears are and why people are afraid; we have seen how fear affects people. Now this is the heart and crux of the whole matter: How can we overcome fear?

There are those who think they can overcome fear by changing their geographical location to Florida, Phoenix, Hollywood or Hawaii. But people in Hollywood and over in Hawaii and down in Florida and out in Phoenix are fear-ridden just like people everywhere else. In fact, these people who have tried to escape by running to another location have discovered that their fears were at the city limits waiting for them when they arrived. You don't run away geographically from fear.

Then there are those who think they can muster up a lot of courage and be the he-man and say, "Fears, be gone! Away with all fears!" But it matters not how long or how loud you speak to them, your fears will not go away in that manner. But I do have good news for you—you can overcome your fears in three very simple steps:

> **Face up to your fear.**

1. **Face up to your fear.** Admit your fear, confess it and acknowledge it. Failure to do so represses it. To repress your fears means you drive them down into your subconscious mind, and they fester and fester until they manifest themselves in all sorts of crazy ideas and illogical, weird behavior. So, if you have a fear, don't repress it; confess it, face up to it.

2. **Replace your fear with faith.** It has been observed that both fear and failure sail into the harbor of your mind, but only faith should be permitted to anchor. One thing no person should ever forget: Beyond human reasoning and beyond human strength, there is a power available to all men—the power of God.

> **Replace your fear with faith.**

Do you know what all the books on psychology do? Do you know what all the material you can read on how to allay and overcome your fears does? From a human standpoint, they tell you that you can replace all your bad thoughts with good thoughts and automatically you will be somebody.

But you and I know we need something beyond human reasoning, beyond human ingenuity, beyond human power, to overcome our fears. And that something is the power of God Himself. Our worries, our anxieties and all things that fret us, that frustrate us, that bother us, can be defeated only by the power of God.

I have a list of seven demons, seven *d*s, that I especially rebuke every day in my devotions: the demons of **discouragement**, of **depression**, of **despondency**, of **despair**, of **deficiency**, of **doubt** and of **defeat**. I rebuke them in the power and in the name of the Lord Jesus Christ. I also include fear, frustration and failure. I'm not here to tell you that I'm never bothered by any of these, but I will tell you that I have learned to overcome through Christ the power of Satan in every one of these demons.

God has the strength you need. God has the wisdom you need. God has the courage you need. God has the patience you need.

But wait! There is but one way you can get from God what you need:

"Ask, and it shall be given you; seek, and ye shall find; knock, and it shall be opened unto you:

"For every one that asketh receiveth; and he that seeketh findeth; and to him that knocketh it shall be opened."—Matt. 7:7, 8.

Replace your fear with faith.

A famous psychiatrist, William Saddler, said, "The only known cure for fear is faith." There is a classic example in Hebrews 11 where the Bible says, "By faith he [Moses] forsook Egypt, not fearing the wrath of the king." Get the picture: **"By faith...not fearing."** Faith and fear are opposite states of mind. If one is controlling your thinking at any given time, the other is not. Your life is being ruled either by faith or by fear.

But you say, "Pastor, my faith is so weak. How can I increase and strengthen my faith?"

Let me answer: not by examining it. You can sit around and examine your faith all day long, but it will not increase. There is but one way to strengthen your faith, and that is by **exercising** it. "Faith cometh by hearing, and hearing by the word of God." Enlarge your capacity for the Book, and you can enlarge your concept of God and of faith.

The road that takes you from fear to faith is prayer, and anyone can travel that road. The psalmist tells us in Psalm 34:4, "I sought the LORD, and he heard me, and delivered me from all my fears." He heard me! I prayed to Him, and He heard me and delivered me from all my fears!

Then Psalm 27:1 says, "The LORD is my light and my salvation; whom shall I fear? the LORD is the strength of my life; of whom shall I be afraid?"

Psalm 46:1 and 2 says, "GOD is our refuge and strength, a very present help in trouble. Therefore will not we fear, though the earth be removed, and though the mountains be carried into the midst of the sea." Do not fear.

Look at Psalm 56, verse 3: "What time I am afraid, I will trust in thee." Verse 4 says, "In God I will praise his word, in God I have put my trust; I will not fear what flesh can do unto me." Then verse 11: "In God have I put my trust: I will not be afraid what man can do unto me."

Isaiah 41:10 admonishes, "Fear thou not; for I am with thee: be not dismayed; for I am thy God: I will strengthen thee; yea, I will help thee; yea, I will uphold thee with the right hand of my righteousness."

Every Christian has two options of what kind of life he wants to live: a first-class life or a second-class life. "What time I am afraid, I will trust in thee" is second-class living—fear, then trust. But you can have a first-class life. Notice the wording of Isaiah 12:2: "I will trust, and not be afraid." Did you get that? Second-class living is when fear comes, then you trust the Lord. First-class living is trusting God, then fear doesn't come. Rich! Wonderful! Fantastic! If it weren't in the Bible, I wouldn't believe it! Get on that first-class boat! Don't wait until fears come and then say, "Lord, here I am; help me." Just say, "Lord, I'm Yours. And I don't expect fear to take over my life, because I'm living first-class."

"Fear not" appears in the Bible 365 times—one time for every day in the year. The Bible says live one day at a time. You can start every day with a fresh, new "fear not." Then that day will be filled with joy, happiness, peace and contentment. You can look the Devil right in the eye and say, "Look, Devil! God said I don't have to fear you today. Go sell your wares to somebody else. I'm living first-class. I'm trusting the Lord."

> Live in honesty with yourself, with others and with God.

Step one: Face up to your fears. Step two: Replace your fear with faith. Step three: **Live in honesty with yourself, with others and with God.**

Step three is more than a simple step; it's a pattern of living. It's more than a formula; it's a philosophy of life. The bottom line of this philosophy is, cultivate the proper love relationship. Love God; love others. Jesus said to do both in Matthew 22:37–39.

> Cultivate the proper love relationship. Love God; love others.

Then I read in I John 4:18, "There is no fear in love; but perfect love [mature love] casteth out fear." That ought to give us a new lease on life.

I said that the bottom line is to cultivate the proper love relationship—loving God and loving others. And the Bible says, "There is no fear in love; but perfect love casteth out fear." If fear does come in, love will knock it down, tie it up, cast it out because fear and love cannot dwell simultaneously. Love always expels fear.

Those who refuse to live within God's circle of love are living in hellish fear, in hellish worry and in hellish anxiety; and the smoke of their torment will ascend up forever and ever.

Trust in God, do good, live honestly, love people, and you have nothing to fear—not even fear itself.

A little girl was running toward the cemetery as the

night fell. Someone said to her, "But aren't you afraid to go through the cemetery at night?"

She answered, "Oh no. My home is just on the other side."

You and I can look at the cemetery; we can look at the awful, awesome enemy of death, and we can say with the psalmist, "Yea, though I walk through the valley of the shadow of death, I will fear no evil: for thou art with me."

If you read this week or next week or next month or next year that Raymond Wesley Barber has slipped out of this life and died and that my remains are in some funeral home, know this: I never feared, because my Home is just on the other side of the grave.

Jesus said, "I am the resurrection, and the life: he that believeth in me, though he were dead, yet shall he live: And whosoever liveth and believeth in me shall never die" (John 11:25,26).

CONCLUSION: When Fear knocks at the door, Faith says, "Nobody is at home."

10.
ATTITUDE OF ANGER

There are two passages of Scripture to which I want you to turn. Both come from the pen of the wisest man who ever lived, with the exception, of course, of our Lord—the wise Solomon.

Our basic passage is Proverbs 23:7:

"For as he thinketh in his heart, so is he."

Then for the message for this hour, "Attitude of Anger," I call your attention to Ecclesiastes 7:9:

"Be not hasty in thy spirit to be angry: for anger resteth in the bosom of fools."

Don't look now, but your attitude is showing.

The word *anger* or *angry* is commonly used in connection with two other words: *frustration* and *aggression*. Generally speaking, when a person is angry, he becomes frustrated, then expresses his frustration in some sort of aggressive behavior.

Anger is a universal emotion. Psychologists divide the human span of life into several stages: the infant (the first two weeks), babyhood (until the end of the second

> Anger is a universal emotion.

year), early childhood, late childhood, adolescence and then maturity.

Psychologists tell us that one of the very first emotions to show up and to express itself, even in babyhood (from the second week to the second year) is anger. The child quickly learns that anger gets the attention he wants. The child ordinarily expresses it by screaming, waving his arms, holding his breath, jumping up and down, throwing himself on the floor, hitting, kicking or even biting. One of the most common ways for a child to vent his anger is to fling across the room whatever he has in his hand. I have been told that when I was a baby and got angry, I always threw the milk bottle.

Now as we grow older and reach some degree of maturity and as we develop chronologically and mentally, anger is generally expressed in a more sophisticated way. As we mature, we express anger in two basic ways: **vocally** and **physically**. When expressing your anger vocally, be careful. "He who has a sharp tongue will soon cut his own throat" is sage advice.

Three basic questions: What is anger? How does anger affect us? How do we overcome anger?

I. WHAT IS ANGER?

The dictionary will tell you that *anger* is "a strong passion or emotion of displeasure excited by a sense of injury or insult."

In the Bible, two Greek words are used for *anger*. One means anger that flares up immediately and burns out just as quickly. The other is the anger that lingers, that seethes inside, that festers and continues over a prolonged period.

There is some value in the capacity to become angry. Some expressions of anger are good and profitable. Even the Apostle Paul admonishes us in Ephesians 4:26, "Be ye angry, and sin not." We should be angry at the Devil. We ought to adopt the little Salvation Army chorus about the Devil:

> **The Devil and me, we don't agree.**
> **I hate him, and he hates me.**

We ought to be angry at all evil forces that are at work in our world. We ought to be angry at any form of hypocrisy, deception or evil. Moses was angry at Pharaoh, Jesus was angry at the Pharisees, Abraham Lincoln was angry at slavery. I'm saying, certain forms of anger are good and profitable.

The philosopher Aristotle said:

> **Anybody can become angry. That is easy; but to be angry at the right person to the right degree at the right time for the right purpose in the right way is not within everybody's power, and not easy.**

We have all discovered that. We have been mad at the wrong time a lot of times, at the wrong people, at the wrong things, for the wrong reasons and to the wrong degree. But controlled anger, the proper kind of anger, is not all that bad.

I will talk about anger that is destructive, bad, detrimental to the body, to the soul, to the mind, to the testimony, to the home, to the family and to society.

Nobody ever promised us that we would be free from hurts, disappointments, defeats, failures, fears or frustrations. Why, then, do we get so all-fired angry when these things come?

If any man had any right or reason to be angry, I believe Job did. You remember the story of Job in the Bible, how everything he had was taken away from him. He lost his sheep. He lost his oxen. He lost his camels. He lost his sons. He lost his daughters. He lost his barns. He lost his crops. He lost everything he had, including his health. And to add insult to injury, his wife said to him, 'Why don't you just curse God and die?' But Job knew there was a purpose in all these things.

Dear friend, everything that comes your way is designed

for a purpose. This is not a world operated by accident. These are not coincidental things. God weaves things into the pattern of your life and program to make you a mature, solid, firm, grown-up, productive Christian. It takes all kinds of experiences, all kinds of things to make us the strong people we desire to be.

If we never faced cold north winds, then we would never be able to stand a storm. God designs even the problems and things that seem unfair for our own good. "And we know that all things work together for good to them that love God, to them who are the called according to his purpose."

Now all of us can, in the face of difficult, bitter, disturbing, disheartening, disillusioning, discouraging times, look at Romans 8:28 and see that all things are working together for our own good and God's own glory.

Job could not do that. That promise of Romans 8:28 had not yet been written; but Job had a sense of value in his heart, knowing that though God took away from him, God would add to him. So Job could say, in response to all his friends and to his wife, "The LORD gave, and the LORD hath taken away; blessed be the name of the LORD," and, "Though he slay me, yet will I trust in him."

Why then should we become angry and frustrated simply because things don't go our way? There are going to be some hurts in life. Along the way somebody is going to hurt you, do you wrong. When this happens, there are four ways you can respond:

(1) You can hurt him more—that's **revenge**. (2) You can hurt him to the same degree—that's **retribution**. (3) You can ignore him—that's **indifference**. (4) You can forgive him— that's **Christianity**. That's the Christ way, the God way, the right way, the Bible way.

Anger is emotional immaturity. Anger is symptomatic of

arrested development somewhere along the way. Anger is a sign of weakness, not of strength. Anger is a selfish manifestation of vengeance.

> **Anger is emotional immaturity.**

Remember that the Bible says, "Vengeance is mine; I will repay, saith the Lord." You and I are not to help God repay. We would make a mess of it. God knows how. Here is a word of caution: Anger can be costly.

A tourist tells of a trip to the Yellowstone National Park. He saw a huge grizzly bear eating garbage at a

> **Anger can be costly.**

very convenient place. The guide informed the group that the grizzly could whip any animal in North America.

That night the tourist noticed there was only one animal that the grizzly bear would permit to sit down beside him. Would you believe it—a skunk! Now the bear resented the skunk, and the bear wanted to get even with the skunk, but he didn't. Why? Because the bear knew the high cost of getting even.

In life there are lots of bears and lots of problems and lots of things to provoke you to anger; but for your sake and your testimony's sake, count the cost of getting even. Remember the skunk.

Originally anger was associated with a picture of a plant that swells up with juice. Now be careful. When you are angry and lashing out at somebody, you might be making a sap of yourself!

Do you want to know the real cause of anger, whether it's in an infant, a baby, young child, older child, adolescent or adult? People get angry when they cannot have their own way. Every source of irritation, every expression of anger, is because you and I have been denied our own selfish way about something.

Only man has the gift of intelligent speech, and he

spends most of his time *growling!* Isn't that strange?

II. HOW DOES ANGER AFFECT US?

You remember the story in the book of Daniel about Nebuchadnezzar, king of Babylon. Nebuchadnezzar had a dream that troubled him. He could not remember it, to say nothing of what it meant. So Nebuchadnezzar called in all the wise men of Babylon, all the soothsayers, all the magi, who were said to be the wisest men on earth. When they could not recount the dream with its interpretation, he issued a decree that all the wise men be put to death.

Question: Was Nebuchadnezzar angry at the wise men of Babylon? Not at all. He didn't dislike those men. Well, what was wrong with Nebuchadnezzar? He had a deep-seated frustration because he couldn't remember a dream, and he took his anger out on somebody else.

A man who goes around all the time lashing out at his wife or at his children or at his boss or at his neighbor or at his friend is not angry with them; he just has a deep-seated frustration. Something is seething, boiling and festering

Anger behaves like a fool.

deep down inside, and it has become a frustration to him; and his aggressive, overt way of showing it is by lashing out at somebody else.

Anger behaves like a fool. "Be not hasty in thy spirit to be angry: for anger resteth in the bosom of fools."

Now, I'm not suggesting that you never will get angry. All of us do.

Somebody says, "I've never really been mad at my wife." Wait a minute, mister! There is something wrong. "I've never been mad at my husband." Wait a minute, lady! There is something wrong. Neither of you is human. We all get angry at someone to some degree or another, but I'm talking about this going around and lashing out. This is the result of a deep-rooted frustration.

Friend, sit down and take inventory of your life and see what's wrong. Don't blame your anger on others. It's not their fault. Look inside—introspection, the psychologists call it. Look within your own heart and see why you are lashing out at people.

Listen to some of the things anger will do to you.

Anger will *disorder your nervous system*.

The little girl said to her mother, "Mother, why is it when you are cross, you say it's your nerves; and when I'm nervous, you say I'm cross?" It depends on which foot the shoe is on, doesn't it?

Not only that, but anger will *shatter your soul*. It injures your friends, it is offensive to God, and it brings out the beast in you.

Two little girls were at play. The family of one had just purchased a new home. She said to her friend, "I want to show you our new house." So she took her into the house. "This is the living room...this is the dining room...this is the kitchen...this is the bedroom...and this one is my bedroom." When they finally ended up in the den, she said, "This is our den, and this is where Daddy spends most of his time. By the way, does your daddy have a den?"

"Oh no," the other said. "He just growls all over the house."

Anger does bring out the beast in us.

How many times have you said, "Boy, I'm going to give him a piece of my mind"? Be careful! You might not have much to spare.

The primary question for the believer is not, How do I let off steam? The primary question for the believer is, How do I prevent steam from building up?

An angry man is seldom reasonable. A reasonable man is seldom angry. When anger enters your heart, it brings a poison with it. Every time you get mad, a poisonous enzyme is secreted into your body. Have you heard people say, "I was so mad I got sick"? That really happens, because a poison is secreted into your body, and people who stay mad all the time usually feel bad all the time. They are tired. They look lifeless, energyless, and they are always complaining of something. Anger is not always the cause, but a person who is constantly angry is not well physically. And certainly he is not well spiritually or emotionally or psychologically.

Anger *leads to rage*. People who fly into a rage always

Anger leads to rage.

make a bad landing. It's easy to get up in the air; it's the coming down that hurts. Some of you know what I mean, for you have been there.

When you are tempted to anger, there are three verses I suggest you read:

(1) The *humility* verse—Job 18:4: "He teareth himself in his anger: shall the earth be forsaken for thee? and shall the rock be removed out of his place?" In other words, do you think the earth is going to change its motion and go to shaking or the rocks are going to get up and start tumbling off the mountainside simply because you are mad? That will bring you down, brother.

(2) The *punishment* verse—Matthew 5:22. Jesus said, "Whosoever is angry with his brother without a cause shall be in danger of the judgment."

(3) The *melting* verse—Proverbs 15:1: "A soft answer turneth away wrath." If you are arguing or lashing out or exchanging harsh words, it is rather difficult to continue if the other person smiles at you. The last part of that verse says, "...but grievous words stir up anger."

When I speak an unkind or hateful or harsh or bitter or

angry word toward you, and you turn right around and speak in like manner to me, that just gets us both all the more stirred up. Then soon I will whip you or get whipped.

I'll never forget the story my daddy tells about my older brother Bob. Bob was always a big, sort-of-overweight fellow. One day he came home from school crying, "Daddy, somebody beat me."

Daddy said, "All right; we'll just go and find out who it is."

Daddy put Bob into the car, and they drove down to the school. There was a husky boy there. Daddy said, "Is that the one?"

Bob said, "No." They drove a bit farther.

Now they saw another fellow. Daddy said, "Is that the guy?"

"No." They drove on. There was a little runt, and Bob said, "There he is."

What I'm saying is, don't continue stirring up anger with harsh words in exchange. "A soft answer turneth away wrath."

III. HOW CAN WE OVERCOME ANGER?

There are a lot of suggestions. Some people bite their tongues or they bite their lips or they count to ten. Thomas Jefferson said, "If you are angry, count to ten; if very angry, to one hundred."

Someone said, "If anger arises in thy heart, instantly seal up thy lips and let it not go forth. For, like fire, when it lacks air, it will soon die out."

Now there are all kinds of things people have offered or suggested—all plausible—for anger, but I believe God's way is best.

Turn to chapter 12 of the book of Romans, verses 17 through 21. This is God's way, which is an absolute guarantee that you can handle and overcome your anger.

"Recompense to no man evil for evil. Provide things honest in the sight of all men.

"If it be possible, as much as lieth in you, live peaceably with all men.

"Dearly beloved, avenge not yourselves, but rather give place unto wrath: for it is written, Vengeance is mine; I will repay, saith the Lord.

"Therefore if thine enemy hunger, feed him; if he thirst, give him drink: for in so doing thou shalt heap coals of fire on his head.

"Be not overcome of evil, but overcome evil with good."

> **Kill your enemy with kindness.**

Did you ever just want to kill somebody? I want to tell you how to do it and get by with it. Kill your enemy with kindness. That's faster than with a 747. I've killed a lot of people that way, and I ought to know. And I suspect I've been killed that way a few times.

> **Overcome evil with good.**

When I find somebody bent on being angry and who is upset and disgruntled with me, I do everything I can to be nice to him. I'm saying, kill people with kindness. It will work. It's God's way. Don't try to overcome evil with evil, but overcome evil with good. Firemen don't use fire to fight fire.

There are three scriptural antidotes to anger: **prayer, love** and **hospitality**. It's hard to be mad at somebody you are praying for. It is hard to stay mad at a person you love. It is very difficult to be mad at somebody and do something good for him at the same time. So prayer, love and hospitality are three strong antidotes to anger, and the Apostle Paul deals with all of them in the verses we just read.

Turn to Matthew's Gospel, the Sermon on the Mount, in Matthew 5:43–45. Jesus also deals with these three actions: prayer, love and hospitality.

"Ye have heard that it hath been said, Thou shalt love thy neighbour, and hate thine enemy.

"But I say unto you, Love your enemies, bless them that curse you, do good to them that hate you, and pray for them which despitefully use you, and persecute you;

"That ye may be the children of your Father which is in heaven."

Prayer, love and hospitality— antidotes to anger.

> Prayer, love and hospitality are strong antidotes to anger.

The poet said:

> He who strives not to stem his anger's tide
> Does a wild horse unbridled ride.

Here are five ways to handle and/or overcome your anger:

1. **Do your best to avoid any situation that may lead to anger.** Colossians 3:8: "Put off all these; anger,..." A number of things are named, but the first one is anger.

2. **When you feel anger coming on, move slowly,** like molasses in January. James 1:19: "Let every man be slow to wrath."

3. **Practice the art of controlling your temper.** Proverbs 16:32: "He that is slow to anger is better than the mighty; and he that ruleth his spirit than he that taketh a city."

4. **Do not allow anger to lead you to sin.** Ephesians 4:26: "Be ye angry, and sin not."

5. **Do not nurse anger.** Ephesians 4:26: "Let not the sun go down on your wrath."

In other words, if you become angry, get over it; get it behind you; get it out of your system. You'll never get over anger if you feed it and nurse it.

It's like a fellow with a sore on his arm. If he goes around pulling back the bandage and saying, "Look at my sore," and another fellow spits tobacco juice on it, it's going to get worse. Just let it get saturated with germs, and it will get worse. And if you nurse anger, it will get worse.

Now let's sum it all up in the words of the Apostle Paul in Ephesians 4:31 and 32:

"Let all bitterness, and wrath, and anger, and clamour, and evil speaking, be put away from you, with all malice:

"And be ye kind one to another, tenderhearted, forgiving one another, even as God for Christ's sake hath forgiven you."

That will do it! By the grace of God and the help of the Holy Spirit, you and I can control and overcome anger.

CONCLUSION: When **anger** rules the head, **sin** reigns in the heart.

11.
ATTITUDE OF UNFORGIVENESS

"For as he thinketh in his heart, so is he."—Prov. 23:7.

You are not what you think you are, but what you *think,* you *are.*

Paul wrote to the church at Philippi, "Let this mind be in you, which was also in Christ Jesus."

Matthew 18:21–35, the text for my message, reads:

"Then came Peter to him, and said, Lord, how oft shall my brother sin against me, and I forgive him? till seven times?

"Jesus saith unto him, I say not unto thee, Until seven times: but, Until seventy times seven.

"Therefore is the kingdom of heaven likened unto a certain king, which would take account of his servants.

"And when he had begun to reckon, one was brought unto him, which owed him ten thousand talents.

"But forasmuch as he had not to pay, his lord commanded him to be sold, and his wife, and children, and all that he had, and payment to be made.

"The servant therefore fell down, and worshipped him, saying, Lord, have patience with me, and I will pay thee all.

"Then the lord [or master] *of that servant was moved with compassion, and loosed him, and forgave him the debt.*

[Now watch this very carefully.]

"But the same servant went out, and found one of his fellow-servants, which owed him an hundred pence: and he laid hands on him,

and took him by the throat, saying, Pay me that thou owest.

"And his fellowservant fell down at his feet, and besought him, saying, Have patience with me, and I will pay thee all.

"And he would not: but went and cast him into prison, till he should pay the debt.

"So when his fellowservants saw what was done, they were very sorry, and came and told unto their lord all that was done.

"Then his lord, after that he had called him, said unto him, O thou wicked servant, I forgave thee all that debt, because thou desiredst me:

"Shouldest not thou also have had compassion on thy fellowservant, even as I had pity on thee?

"And his lord was wroth, and delivered him to the tormentors, till he should pay all that was due unto him.

"So likewise shall my heavenly Father do also unto you, if ye from your hearts forgive not every one his brother their trespasses."

More than any other story in the New Testament, this story sets forth clearly, unmistakably and concisely the law of forgiveness on your part and mine.

Let's get the story. Here is a master who owns a lot of servants. One owed him a huge sum of money. It was the law that if a man could not pay his debts, he would be cast into prison. If necessary, his wife and children and all he had would be sold to settle the debt.

When this man was brought in, he said to his master, "I don't have it. If you will be patient with me, I will pay you in time." His master, moved with compassion, forgave him and canceled the debt.

This same servant who had been forgiven found one of his fellowservants who was indebted to him and owed him a small sum of money. Because his fellowservant could not pay it, he had the man's goods sold, and he put him in prison and had him held there until he could pay it all.

When the master heard about what that servant had

done, he was very angry and called this man in and said, "Wait a minute! You owed me a huge sum of money. You asked me to be patient with you. I felt sorry for you, I forgave you, and I canceled the debt. Should you not have done the same thing for your servant that I did for you? Should you not have had pity, compassion and mercy? Should you not have forgiven him just like I forgave you?"

And then Jesus put the clincher on the whole thing: "Likewise shall my heavenly Father do also unto you, if ye from your hearts forgive not every one his brother their trespasses."

That's an amazing story! The bottom line is, if you and I are not willing to forgive those who have wronged us, God will not forgive us.

The ugliest sight on earth is a Christian full of animosity and bitterness toward a fellow Christian. An unforgiving attitude is the most soul-destroying practice of which a person can be guilty. I'm convinced that one of the very first things that is going to show up at the judgment seat of Christ will be that ugly, unforgiving spirit.

Don't look now, but your attitude is showing!

I. FORGIVENESS: A BASIC PRINCIPLE

Three things about forgiveness:

First, forgiveness is the basic principle upon which the Christian Faith is founded. Someone said the two distinguishing marks of a Christian are giving and forgiving. In the Garden of Eden, a wedge was driven between God and man. That wedge is called sin. At the precise moment, God Almighty offered a plan for man's redemption. This scheme of redemption is

> Forgiveness is the basic principle upon which the Christian Faith is founded.

based on one principle—forgiveness. It is as though God said, having recorded the sin of Adam and Eve in the garden, "Here is what I will do: I will send My Son to die on the cross, and all who believe in Him will be forgiven."

So Jesus Christ came. He died on the cross. He offered forgiveness and reconciliation to all men. "Reconcile" or "reconciliation" is mentioned several times in the Scriptures. It is used in a different sense altogether in II Corinthians 5:18, 19. Ordinarily in the New Testament where the word is mentioned, it suggests two people at odds with each other moving simultaneously together, coming for forgiveness—a coming together.

"And all things are of God, who hath reconciled us to himself by Jesus Christ, and hath given to us the ministry of reconciliation;

"To wit, that God was in Christ, reconciling the world unto himself, not imputing their trespasses unto them; and hath committed unto us the word of reconciliation."

In these verses, and in this context, the word "reconcile" means something a little different. Here you and I are—sinful, stubborn, rebellious, antagonistic, full of iniquity and shame, at odds *with* God and at a distance *from* God. Here God condescended and came down in the Person of His Son to reconcile us unto Himself. We did not reach up to get God. It was not two parties moving simultaneously toward the goal of coming together. It was God moving toward man, reconciling us to Himself.

So God has forgiven our sins. God loved, so God forgave. From the cross our Lord cried, "Father, forgive them; for they know not what they do."

I repeat, forgiveness is the basic principle upon which the whole structure of the Christian Faith is built.

II. BIBLICAL PRINCIPLES

Now the second thing about forgiveness: **forgiveness must be in accord with biblical principles.** Three questions are to be answered at this point under this heading:

> **Forgiveness must be in accord with biblical principles.**

Question 1: *What should I forgive?* I mean, if a guy comes up and knocks me down, am I to forgive him? If a guy spits in my face, am I to forgive him? Well, let's just see what Jesus did.

Do you know the kind of people who harmed Jesus? Do you know what they did to Him? They called Him an illegitimate child. They spit in His face. They plucked out His beard. They blasphemed Him. They cursed Him. They put a robe of mockery on Him. They smote Him upon the face. They lied about Him. They criticized Him. They did everything you can imagine to Jesus. Now watch this: He prayed, "Father, forgive them."

Now if someone has hated you, lied about you, criticized you or cheated you, you **can** and **must** forgive him. I'm saying, forgiveness must be carried out along biblical guidelines. You know what you have to forgive—anything and everything that is done against you.

Question 2: *How often should I forgive?* Now some of you may be saying, "What's the use of my forgiving him if he is going to turn right around and offend me again?" Well, Jesus gave the answer to that:

"Take heed to yourselves: If thy brother trespass against thee, rebuke him; and if he repent, forgive him.

"And if he trespass against thee seven times in a day, and seven times in a day turn again to thee, saying, I repent; thou shalt forgive him."—Luke 17:3, 4.

Now back to my text. Peter had asked in verse 21, 'How many times shall I forgive my brother? Seven times?'

Seven is the number of divine completion in the Bible. In the book of Revelation, for example, we find: seven spirits of God, seven eyes, seven angels, seven trumpets, seven vials of judgment and on and on. The number seven is the number of ultimate, divine perfection and completion.

Peter said, 'Lord, how many times must I forgive that fellow who wrongs me? Seven times?'

Jesus answered, "I say not unto thee, Until seven times: but, Until seventy times seven"—490 times. You might be asking, "Am I to take that number absolutely literally? If so, well…487, 488, 489—just one more time, then I can sock him in the nose."

Let me say something to you: If you are counting, you are not forgiving. Seventy times seven is an ultimate, indefinite, incalculable number of times. On and on we are to forgive. By the time you have forgiven a man that many times, you would be in an attitude of forgiveness.

The poet said:

> O God, my sins are manifold;
>   Against my life they cry.
> And all my guilty deeds foregone,
>   Up to Thy temple fly.
>
> Wilt Thou release my trembling soul
>   That to despair is driven?
> "Forgive," a blessed voice replied,
>   "And thou shalt be forgiven."
>
> I gave them due benevolence;
>   They spurned me in their pride.
> They render evil for my good;
>   My patience they deride.

Arise, my King, and be thou proud,
And righteous ruin deal them.
"Forgive," the awful answer came,
"As thou wouldst be forgiven."

Seven times, O Lord, I pardoned them.
Seven times they've sinned again.
They practice still to work me woe
And triumph in my pain.

But let them dread my vengeance now,
To just resentment driven.
"Forgive," the voice in thunder spake,
"Or never be forgiven."

If you and I are not willing to continue unendingly, unceasingly, innumerably, incalculably to forgive those who have wronged us, we cannot be forgiven.

Question 3: *Who is to take the initiative in forgiveness?* Here is where it gets down to the nitty-gritty. Here is where the rubber meets the road.

Someone put it this way: "A more gracious victory cannot be gained over another man than this, that when the injury began on his part, the forgiveness should begin on ours." In other words, when the other person is wrong, we are to initiate forgiveness. That's just to say, both logically and scripturally, only one person is responsible to be the first to forgive, and that person is you. By that we mean, if someone has wronged you, you should initiate the reconciliation.

That is what God did. We wronged Him; He initiated the reconciliation. This is precisely what II Corinthians 5:19 says. We are rebellious, stubborn, obstinate and sinful—and God comes down to reconcile us. We didn't initiate the movement of reconciliation.

So I ask you a question: inasmuch as the moment man offended God, God moved in his direction to forgive him, then what better example can we follow than the divine example?

To err is human; to forgive is divine. Someone wrote,

> To err is human; to forgive is divine.

"Forgiveness is the perfume that the trampled flower casts upon the heel that crushed it." Isn't that beautiful? I'm talking about a divine example. I'm talking about what you and I are supposed to do.

I asked the question: Who is to initiate? The answer is—we are. Ephesians 4:32 says, "And be ye kind one to another, tenderhearted, forgiving one another, even as God for Christ's sake hath forgiven you." In other words, Paul is saying to the church at Ephesus and to us today, "Since God through Christ has so freely forgiven you, you are to forgive the one who has wronged you."

In Colossians 3:13 Paul says, "Forbearing one another, and forgiving one another, if any man have a quarrel against any: even as Christ forgave you, so also do ye."

I read about a revival meeting where not one soul had been saved; not one single move had been made. Two members were at odds with each other, and they sat on opposite sides of the church. They sang the same hymns, gave in the same offering plate, worshiped in the same place. They sat in the revival meeting and heard the Word of God, but they were so mad at each other that they wouldn't speak.

Then on the second night before the closing, they got things fixed, and a revival came. The greatest revival that church had ever known came because two stubborn, hard-headed, backslidden Christians decided they were no longer going to act like the Devil but start acting like Christ and learn to forgive.

Do you want to know why revival is not coming? It may

be that you have a deep-seated hatred, bitterness or unforgiving spirit against somebody. God can't and won't bless a situation like that. We will hinder the blessings of God until we can shake hands, smile and say, "I love you. I forgive you" for whatever has happened. When a friend makes a mistake, don't rub it in; rub it out.

> Forgiveness must be carried out along biblical guidelines.

I'm saying, forgiveness must be carried out along biblical guidelines.

III. SERIOUS CONSEQUENCES

My third point is (and this is the heart of the whole matter): **Failure to forgive results in very serious consequences.**

Before I get into the four basic consequences, let me just say this: You cannot have a good, sound, physically healthy body if you have resentments and grudges in your heart.

> You cannot have the freedom to face the person you hold a grudge against.

Now, the first serious consequence: *You cannot have the freedom to face the person you hold a grudge against.* It is both unwholesome and unholy for a Christian to have personal enemies and hold personal resentments and grudges against anybody. It is both unhealthy and unspiritual. In such a condition, when you meet that certain person, your blood begins to boil and your temper flares.

Did you ever see someone coming down the street and cross over to the other side to keep from speaking to him? Did you ever see someone coming down a church aisle and cross over to the other aisle to keep from speaking to that person? Unwillingness and failure to forgive render you absolutely incapable of meeting that person face-to-face.

If you attend the funeral of someone you have said some unkind things about or mistreated, you sit there, and the pangs of conscience keep on gnawing with every word.

John and Bill, two young boys, were sharing the same hospital room. They had argued for several days and said some terribly unkind things to each other. One night as the nurse was preparing John's bed for him, John said to her, "That old Bill is a real meany. I will never forgive him as long as I live."

The nurse said, "Now, John, it's not right for you to feel that way. Suppose you die in the night. You would be sorry that you never forgave Bill."

John thought about it very seriously for a few moments, then said, "Well, all right. If I die in the night, I will forgive him. But if I don't die, Bill had better watch out in the morning!"

Strange how "religious" some folks get on their deathbeds, isn't it?

Folks, it's not a matter of saying, "Well, Lord, if You are going to strike me out, rub me out, erase me, I'll forgive."

While living, you had better be ready to forgive, or you won't have the freedom to face that person. A forgiving Christian need never feel two-faced when meeting anyone anywhere.

And when you forgive, forget. If you go around telling people how much or how many you have forgiven, chances are you haven't either forgiven or forgotten.

When men bury mad dogs, they don't leave the tail sticking up out of the ground. When the hatchet is buried, bury the handle also. Strike the record clean. Let bygones be bygones. Very serious consequences result if you don't.

The second serious consequence is this: *You have no*

freedom to worship if you are not willing to forgive.

Turn to Matthew 5:23 and 24. There Jesus says:

"Therefore if thou bring thy gift to the altar [if you come into worship, is what it really means], *and there rememberest that thy brother hath ought against thee;*

> You have no freedom to worship if you are not willing to forgive.

"Leave there thy gift before the altar, and go thy way; first be reconciled to thy brother, and then come and offer thy gift."

By the way, did God tell you to stuff your offering back in your pocket? No! He said leave your gift before the altar and go be reconciled to your brother. Then come and offer your gift. There is no freedom to worship until we are willing to forgive.

The third consequence: *You have no freedom to pray if you are not willing to forgive.*

Look at Mark 11:25 and 26:

> You have no freedom to pray if you are not willing to forgive.

"And when ye stand praying, forgive, if ye have ought against any: that your Father also which is in heaven may forgive you your trespasses.

"But if ye do not forgive, neither will your Father which is in heaven forgive your trespasses."

You have no freedom to pray unless you are willing to forgive. By the way, husband, you can't have an open, clear channel to Heaven if you are mistreating your wife.

"Likewise, ye husbands, dwell with them according to knowledge, giving honour unto the wife, as unto the weaker vessel, and as being heirs together of the grace of life; that your prayers be not hindered."— I Pet. 3:7.

There are serious consequences of unforgiving spirits.

Consequence four: *You have no freedom to ask God to forgive you if you aren't willing to forgive others.*

Look at Matthew 6:14 and 15:

You have no freedom to ask God to forgive you if you aren't willing to forgive others.	*"For if ye forgive men their trespasses, your heavenly Father will also forgive you:* *"But if ye forgive not men their trespasses, neither will your Father forgive your trespasses."*

In other words, if you are not willing to forgive others who have wronged you, God will not forgive you.

Then Luke 6:37 says, "Judge not, and ye shall not be judged: condemn not, and ye shall not be condemned: forgive, and ye shall be forgiven."

Forgiveness cannot flow *toward* you until it flows *from* you. You have to forgive if you are going to be forgiven. He who cannot forgive others breaks the bridge over which he himself must pass.

A lot of Christians have a bad case of "grudge-itis." That is a deep-seated, unforgiving spirit against somebody else. Isn't that sad? How unchristian, how un-Christlike it is for us to hold grudges and resentments against our fellow Christians!

I've told you four serious consequences: no freedom to meet the person against whom you hold a grudge on the street, no freedom to worship, no freedom to pray, and no freedom to ask God to forgive you of your own sins, if you are not willing to forgive.

Now let me give you a little spiritual exercise:

Step 1. Pretend there is no one here but you.

Step 2. Clear your mind of all thoughts. Just put your brain in neutral.

Step 3. Take sixty seconds to think whether you know of

one single, solitary person anywhere that you have any animosity toward.

Step 4. Resolve this moment that you are going to make things right with that person as soon as possible.

If you are not willing to do that, you are worse off for coming to church tonight than if you had stayed at home.

12.
ATTITUDE OF PROCRASTINATION

The basic and primary verse for this series of messages is Proverbs 23:7:

"For as he thinketh in his heart, so is he."

We have been dealing with the mind. We pointed you to the book of Philippians, for example, as an illustration of the amount of space God gives in His Holy Record dealing with the mind. Philippians is known as the psychology book of the Bible. There we have that exciting, challenging verse where Paul says, "Let this mind be in you, which was also in Christ Jesus" (2:5). Paul talks about the renewing of the mind day by day. Remember, you are not what you think you are, but what you *think*, you *are*.

The text for my message is Jeremiah 8:20:

"The harvest is past, the summer is ended, and we are not saved."

All through the hot, steaming, sultry, summer nights of June, July and August, we have been singing, praying and preaching. Every song that has been sung, every prayer that has been offered, every message that has been delivered has called for the dedication of your time, your talent and your energy to Christ. The old, old story has been told again and again. But I have a longing to tell it again. If I were to ask how many would once again like to hear the old, old story, every hand in this auditorium would go up.

I remember my paternal grandmother, Granny Stone.

She used to come and visit us. We loved to hear her sing. She would tell us the history of the hymns in the hymnbook. One was about the little Gypsy boy who lay dying. Then she would sing that song:

> Into the tent where a Gypsy boy lay,
> Dying alone at the close of the day.

She would sing every verse. We would say, "Granny, sing that chorus again."

> Tell it again! Tell it again!
> Salvation's story repeat o'er and o'er;
> Till none can say of the children of men,
> "Nobody ever has told me before."

Almost two thousand years ago, outside the walls of the ancient city of Jerusalem, they led the Son of God to the summit of Calvary's mountain, and there they crucified Him. Oh, they drove the spikes into His hands and feet and plunged the sword into His side.

He cried, "Father, forgive them; for they know not what they do." He cried in the end, "Father, into thy hands I commend my spirit: and having said thus, he gave up the ghost."

Though all of these things have been told Sunday after Sunday, yet tragically, fearfully, some are still lost. "The harvest is past, the summer is ended, and we are not saved."

I want to share with you two basic thoughts about the attitude of procrastination:

Procrastination Is Foolish

Procrastination is *foolish*, even in our social and spiritual interactions. We are prone to put off things we know we ought to do. How many times have we said, "Well, someday I'm going to make that visit" or "Someday

Procrastination is foolish.

126

I'm going to write that letter" or "Someday I'm going to bake a cake"?

The poet said:

> Someday—I'm going down the street
> And sit and chat with one whose feet
> Have had to pause and rest awhile
> Before they travel that last mile:
> Well—someday.
>
> Someday—a cake or pie I'll bake,
> And with a cheery smile, I'll take
> It to a home where there is need,
> Just folks of quite a different creed:
> Well—someday!
>
> Someday—a letter I will send
> To that distant, lonely friend;
> I'll tell her every little thing
> That will joy and comfort bring:
> Well—someday.
>
> Someday—a quiet place I'll seek
> Where I can hear my Father speak,
> Where I can listen undisturbed
> To His precious, guiding Word:
> Well—someday.
>
> Someday—I'll surely take the time
> To tell some soul of love divine,
> Of salvation full and free,
> Meant for them as well as me:
> Well—someday.
>
> Someday—I said it long ago.
> The days slip by, and well I know
> "Someday" will never come until

**Today bends to my Father's will.
Why not today?**

In the physical realm, many have experienced this:

One night you woke up with a throbbing toothache. By morning, it had finally eased off, and you got a few winks of sleep. Then it was up and to work. It didn't hurt all day. You thought, *I've got to go to the dentist;* but it didn't hurt for awhile, so you didn't go. Several weeks went by, then several months. Every once in awhile you had just a little quickie feeling there, especially when you bit into something that had tin foil on it. When it got on that tooth, it felt like you got ten thousand volts of electricity. But as soon as you got over that and the tooth got back to normal, you said, *One of these days I'm going to the dentist. He will deaden it, drill a little bit and put filling in, and I'll be all right.*

Finally, after several nights of sleeplessness, you did go to the dentist. He said, "I'm sorry, but I have to pull that tooth."

I'm speaking from experience. I passed out in the dentist's chair! You know, the next time I had a toothache and a bad problem, I went to my dentist. He said, "I believe I'll send you to another dentist to pull this one."

I'm talking about postponing, procrastinating, putting off.

In the book of Acts is a story of a governor by the name of Felix. Paul reasoned with him in three primary areas: of righteousness, of temperance, of judgment to come. And Felix stood there trembling. He said, "Paul, I believe you are right. You've touched me. Something happened here, but, Paul, I've got so many other things to do. I'm the governor, and in this important position, I just believe I had better put it off." He didn't say it exactly in these words, but he said, "Go thy way for this time; when I have a convenient season, I will call for thee" (Acts 24:25).

Now watch the foolishness of this. Here was a powerful,

prominent, polished man who had everything going for him, but he neglected the most important matter in all his life—the salvation of his never-dying soul. He was time-wise but eternity-foolish.

I've searched through the remaining chapters in the book of Acts, and I've searched on into the New Testament hoping and praying somewhere I might find that Felix had a more convenient season, but I've searched in vain. I never found the record where Felix ever had a more convenient time to get right with God.

There is no better time than now to get right with God. There may never be a more convenient time, because God's time is always *present*.

I read in Isaiah 1:18, "Come *now*, and let us reason together, saith the LORD." Jesus said, "Come; for all things are *now* ready." The Apostle Paul said, "*Now* is the day of salvation." Again Paul wrote, "*To day* if ye will hear his voice, harden not your hearts." This is the hour, for God said, "My spirit shall not always strive with man."

You might get by with postponing, procrastinating, in some of the issues of your physical or social life; but it is a foolish thing to think you can procrastinate, put off the decision that is so pressing on your heart and your mind this very moment.

To procrastinate, I believe, is foolish for three reasons: (1) It is often an unconscious process. You are totally unconscious of delaying and postponing the most important thing. (2) If you persist in procrastinating, it will bring you to everlasting ruin. (3) Procrastination not only affects your life, but it affects the lives of those about you and might ultimately result in their eternal damnation.

There is a time I know not when,
A place I know not where,

That marks the destiny of men
To Heaven or despair.

There is a line by man unseen
That crosses every path;
That makes the difference between
God's mercy and His wrath.

If we could visit the regions of the damned, we could probably hear Felix crying out for a more convenient season, but it will never come. Every man who followed Jesus in the New Testament record followed Him on the very first invitation. It is utterly foolish to procrastinate.

Procrastination Is Fatal

Not only is it foolish to procrastinate, but to procrastinate is *fatal*.

Luke 12 tells about a man who thought he had all the time he needed. God called him a fool. Any man who thinks he has all the time he needs is a fool in God's sight. God is over all looking down. He's the Creator. He has time in His own measure, in His own wisdom, in His own guidance. God is not unaware of how much time you have to live. Is it threescore and ten? or maybe fourscore? Who knows? The rich fool said, as he surveyed his lands and barns, 'Why, these barns I have are not big enough. I will pull them down and build greater barns. I will say to my soul, Soul, thou hast much goods laid up for many years; take thine ease, eat, drink, and be merry.'

> Procrastination is fatal.

Man! He thought he had it made! He went to bed that night, just like he always did; but like a bolt of lightning from the sky, there came the voice of the Almighty: "Thou fool, this night thy soul shall be required of thee: then whose shall those things be, which thou hast provided?"

My friend, when the perspiration of death is upon your

brow and the doctors have turned to the family and said it's all over, it won't matter then how many barns you had or how big your house was or the kind of car you drove or the type clothes you wore or how much money you had in the bank or how many zeros were in your salary. "Then whose shall those things be?" The only thing that will matter then is your relationship to God through Jesus Christ alone.

I have an idea that this rich fool not only thought he had all the time in the world, but he thought, *My, I'm important! I'm a big fellow. Nobody can fill my shoes.* I wonder if any of us have ever thought that. I wonder if any of us have said, "Well, nobody can replace me. I'm indispensable." I'll tell you how indispensable you are. Go home and fill your bathtub with water, stick your finger in it, then pull it out. All that water you displaced will show you how important you are. The only really important thing is a personal, heart-to-heart relationship with Christ.

I say, procrastination is fatal! This man kept saying, "I," "me," "my," "my soul." Who said it was *your* soul, my friend? "My" barn. Who said it was *your* barn? "Well, my house and my car are in my name. So I suppose they are mine." No, they are not. If you're a Christian, it all belongs to God. If you are unsaved, the Devil's crowd is going to get it if you don't get saved. When they wheel you out of the room and into the cold storage, somebody else will be rattling your keys; somebody else will be driving your car; somebody else will be wearing your clothes; somebody else will soon be living in your house. You cannot afford to say "my" and "mine" and "I," because it is God's.

It's fatal to procrastinate. The Bible tells us that that very night this man, who deceived himself into thinking he had many years to live, died. Death was then knocking at his door. "It is appointed unto men once to die, but after this the judgment." Death is certain.

I'm glad that death is not the end. We don't die like a beast. After death, we have to face God. For the unbeliever, death means it's all over as far as being saved is concerned. Forever that person will be lost who dies in his sin. Jesus said, 'If you die in your sins, where I am, there you cannot come.'

But there is another side to that coin. For the believer, death is not the end but an entrance into a better world. Paul said, 'To be absent from the body is to be present with the Lord.' One day, after all the tears have been shed around yonder grave, when the trumpet of God sounds, the dead in Christ shall rise.

Friend, if you are not saved and if you keep saying "next week," "next month," "next year," "tomorrow," you will be shut out of Heaven forever.

> **You have no promise of tomorrow.**

There are three reasons that procrastination is fatal:

(1) *You have no promise of tomorrow.* Proverbs 27:1 says, "Boast not thyself of to morrow; for thou knowest not what a day may bring forth."

(2) *You are but one heartbeat away from death.* I read in Proverbs 29:1, "He, that being often reproved hardeneth his neck, shall suddenly be destroyed, and that without remedy."

> **You are but one heartbeat away from death.**

(3) *To gamble with eternity and lose is to be lost forever.*

Revelation 14:11 says, "And the smoke of their torment ascendeth up for ever and ever."

> **To gamble with eternity and lose is to be lost forever.**

Listen as I read these words in Revelation 20:

"And I saw a great white throne, and him that sat on it, from whose face the earth and

the heaven fled away; and there was found no place for them.

"And I saw the dead, small and great, stand before God; and the books were opened: and another book was opened, which is the book of life: and the dead were judged out of those things which were written in the books, according to their works.

"And the sea gave up the dead which were in it; and death and hell delivered up the dead which were in them: and they were judged every man according to their works.

"And death and hell were cast into the lake of fire. This is the second death.

"And whosoever was not found written in the book of life was cast into the lake of fire."—Vss. 11–15.

Procrastination, putting it off until a more convenient season—until next week, until the fall and harvest—is fatal as well as foolish.

One of a famous evangelist's associates tells the story that in 1957 they were driving down the street in New York City. The newspaper boy was on the street corner hollering, "Extra! Extra! Jimmy Dorsey commits suicide."

The associate said the evangelist fell back in the seat of the car and said, "O dear me! Just two days ago Jimmy Dorsey called me on the telephone and said, 'I need to see you so badly.' And I said, 'Jimmy, I'm so busy, and my schedule is so crowded. I'll have to put it off until next week.'"

And the evangelist said, "Oh, if I had just taken a few moments, Jimmy Dorsey might still be alive."

If the need is pressing, if somebody needs you and wants you, don't put it off. It may be too late next week.

If God has spoken to you and if the Holy Spirit is convicting your soul, don't put off your salvation. Next Sunday may be too late. To procrastinate is to be lost forever. Please don't let it happen to you!

> **To procrastinate is to be lost forever.**